Hold Me Tight and Tango Me Home

Hold Me Tight
and Tango Me Home

MARIA FINN

ALGONQUIN BOOKS OF CHAPEL HILL 2010

Published by
ALGONQUIN BOOKS OF CHAPEL HILL
Post Office Box 2225
Chapel Hill, North Carolina 27515-2225

a division of
WORKMAN PUBLISHING
225 Varick Street
New York, New York 10014

While the people and events described in the following pages are real,
some names have been changed for the sake of privacy and, in a few places,
the chronology has been changed to fit the narrative.

Library of Congress Cataloging-in-Publication Data
  Dominguez, Maria Finn.
    Hold me tight and tango me home / Maria Finn. — 1st ed.
      p. cm.
    ISBN 978-1-56512-517-9
    1. Tango (Dance) — Argentina.   2. Dominguez, Maria Finn.   I. Title.
    GV1796.T3.D66 2009
    793.330982 — dc22   2009029855

10 9 8 7 6 5 4 3 2 1
First Edition

For my mother, Beth Paula Finn
(May 26, 1942–May 3, 2009)

Before it was an orgiastic deviltry;
today it is a way of walking.

—JORGE LUIS BORGES, "History of the Tango"

CONTENTS

Hold Me Tight and Tango Me Home

PROLOGUE

WHILE WALKING ALONG the Central Park promenade one Saturday afternoon, I came across a group of people in the most unlikely pairings—a Nubian beauty towered above a man with thick red sideburns, a woman with jet-black hair and the layered skirts and bangles of a gypsy fortune teller was in the arms of a kid in baggy hip-hop pants. A wiry Asian man in crisply pressed pants took the hand of a tiny elderly woman in a shamelessly age-inappropriate mini skirt. I tried to interpret their facial expressions. Focused, serious, wistful, content, melancholic. I stared in fascination. How could they do this? In public, no less.

Tango music scratched out of a boom box as each couple moved in perfect unison. The pairs formed a small circle, as if in orbit around an imaginary axis, stepping, pausing, cutting fractals as they danced, oblivious to the people passing by with curious glances or even those of us who stopped to gape. When the song ended, a man who had been dancing smoothed his hands over his black vest, flashed me a smile, and came over to chat.

"Do you tango?" he asked.

I laughed and said, "No, never."

"You should consider it," he answered. "It's my great passion in life." He explained that initially he attended several lessons a week, then started going to socials every night.

I asked why he'd started dancing.

"My seven-year-old daughter wanted to know why her mother and I divorced. I didn't know. And I couldn't explain how you can love someone so much, then split so far apart. So I began tango to learn how to be with a woman without expecting anything. How to find balance with another person."

He offered a quick lesson and I accepted. First I had to lean against him—I had to trust the lead entirely. I could smell the nape of his neck, feel the slight slope of his shoulders and the soft pulse of his heart. It quickly felt suffocating, and such closeness made me squeamish. He showed me how to step around him while my chest stayed aligned with his. But I was too uncomfortable to be so near someone I didn't know.

Yet I couldn't help but linger when he returned to the group. The tango songs were laments of heartbreak, but the dancers brought to mind the perfect state of bliss. I thought of the perfect completeness described in Aristophanes' Speech from Plato's *Symposium*: People were once whole, but because they didn't properly honor the gods, they were split apart and doomed to be forever searching for their other half. To find one's missing half is to once again experience harmony and happiness. That's what the dancers in Central Park looked like—finally reunited.

Maybe, I thought, I could learn tango if I were with a man I loved. But not with total strangers.

I'd never been more wrong.

CHAPTER 1

El Abrazo, The Embrace

ON THE FIRST night I went to a tango lesson, an occasional breeze, redolent of brackish river water, drifted over the docks. I stood on the coarse wooden planks as the evening light softened and ships silently slipped by. The masts of old wooden schooners and their zig zagging rigging created a theatrical backdrop for the crowd gathering outside New York's South Street Seaport for tango lessons before the social dance started.

In the center of the group a poised man with slicked-back hair began speaking as if he'd said this a thousand times yet still struggled to get his point across. As if it were perfectly natural and also a matter of life or death—that we must first and foremost understand the embrace. A slim, dark-haired woman joined him. They were going to teach an introduction to tango to the random gang of New Yorkers scuffling around them. Tango, in its strictest definition, is a form of music and dance.

In essence, though, it is a way of being—and it lures you, maybe by a phone call or by an e-mail you weren't meant to see; it pulls you from the job that's too staid; it beckons on a night when you're feeling lonely; it promises escape from the grind of daily life. Tango is a journey for those who want their lives to change course; and for others, like me, who believe that their lives have ended, it's an attempt to start living again.

"The tango is about connection. And the way you do this is with the embrace," our teacher began. "There are two main points of connection: your arms and your hands. Through these, you will create and maintain your frame." His partner demonstrated by lifting her arm into the air and gracefully letting it settle on the nape of his neck. Despite the gentleness of her motion, her entire body participated in this single, simple gesture. The bending of her thin arms showed the grooves and ridges of her muscles, and beneath her billowing indigo skirt, her calf muscles flexed.

"And followers, feel your back connect to your fingertips," she said. "Respect the present, be engaged. You're both an individual and part of a pair, contributing fifty percent of everything."

"This is your second point of connection," the instructor said. "Your hands here."

He held his hand open, inviting her to put her hand into his; then they pressed their palms together. "The man must make the woman feel comfortable and protected."

"Don't lean on the man," the woman added. "You always

carry your own weight. And the leader, always give her enough time. Don't hurry her. That way"—she paused and smiled slightly—"she feels beautiful."

"Okay, everyone take a partner," he said.

As in musical chairs, people shifted, rotated, men approached women and held out their hands. The basis of their selections—height, age, beauty, proximity, maybe uncritical eyes or an understanding smile—was a mystery to me.

Some of the couples were clearly on dates. They bickered over who had the embrace right or wrong or who was pushing or pulling too tightly or too softly; others, unable to hold the distance between them, botched the embrace with sloppy kissing. Most of the people who gathered here, though, were strangers; mismatched partners, their styles, heights, and ages incongruous. They were not looking much at each other but standing straight, at attention, waiting for the next order.

I stood by myself. In the shuffle, I and a few other females hadn't moved fast enough, and there just weren't enough men to go around. The old saying "It takes two to tango" is true, especially when it comes to the embrace, and I wasn't going to stand there and practice hugging the air. I went to the bar, ordered a margarita, and took a few sips, wanting numbness but getting a cold headache instead.

I watched the couples moving their shoulders by twisting their torsos, keeping their chests aligned and their legs rooted to the ground. I hated being there without a partner. In our first year of marriage, my husband and I had gone out almost every Saturday night to a club in our neighborhood and danced to Latin music. I had loved showing up with my dance partner, working up a sweat, and going home with my husband. My days of waiting, of hoping to be asked by men to dance salsa, had ended. And those weekly rituals were good for us — dancing was a conversation that never became an argument. We stepped together, broke apart, then found our way back, moving in sync with each other while the crowd pulsed around us. Now I was alone again.

The sky darkened and red neon lights from the Watchtower Building across the water in Brooklyn bled onto the East River. More experienced dancers started to fill the docks, getting ready for the *milonga* to start. (I would come to learn that many *milongas*, or social dances, offered a lesson before the actual dance began.) I stood on the sideline, content to watch. Some people tangoed quickly and maneuvered complicated steps. They wore loose, comfortable clothing and challenged each other. Others held their partners tightly and moved in slow, subtle synchronicity. I noticed their facial expressions, especially the women's. Again I saw some wistfulness, but every once in a while a certain woman passed by with her eyes closed, wearing a slight smile on her face, as if she were experiencing a lovely dream. That sensation was so alien to me right then that I almost hated her for it.

When men asked me to dance, I refused, explaining that I didn't know how. Still, I didn't leave. The music played right to me—the melodies and harmonies of the violin, flute, guitar, *bandoneón*, and piano mourned the maladies of the heart. The classic song "Volver" by Carlos Gardel particularly struck me. He pulled the notes that emphasized the inescapable pain of betrayal that stretches on and transforms into bitter melancholy and finally a bruised heart. The song came to an end with the lyrics *"Vivir / con el alma aferrada / a un dulce recuerdo / que lloro otra vez."* (To live / with the soul clutched / to a sweet memory / that I cry once again.)

Tango understood my broken heart.

I spotted Marcel, a man I knew from salsa dancing. He insisted I dance with him.

"Hey, where's your husband?" he asked.

Tears welled up in my eyes. "It's over," I told him.

"I've been divorced," he answered. "I'm sorry. It's awful." Then he took me in his arms and helped me with the embrace.

Marcel is not someone I would have noticed on the street and considered strikingly good looking, but he was attractive. He had thick lips and soft brown eyes whose lids drooped slightly. There was something about him—his deep voice, his natural warmth and wide, solid chest—that made him more handsome than he appeared at first glance. He also had a girlfriend who danced, so his attention was not romantic.

"There's close embrace, like this," he said, pulling me to him so my arm reached all the way across his shoulders, my hand resting on the slope between his neck and shoulder. "When dance floors get really crowded, you have to stay close and keep all the steps subtle. But if there's room for bigger or longer steps, you need to be in open embrace." He stepped away from me and we slid apart until my hand lay on his bicep. "Either way, we never lose the connection with our arms, but the most important one happens between our chests."

He started walking forward and I stepped backward, moving slowly while he talked me through the steps. "Just relax," he said. "Move to the pace I set. Okay, good."

I felt warmth from his upper torso go straight into my chest, my solar plexus, my stomach, and the leaden feeling inside me softened. I could feel the dark, gaping hole — the deadness I had felt since learning of my husband's affair — and I let the heat coming from this man fill that void. The second song started, and I became aware of Marcel's arms around me: He supported my hand in his and kept the circle of connection, but it was the other arm I really felt, the one wrapped around my back that held me to him and made me feel secure and cared-for. By the third song, I had started to sense his pulse, and for a moment, with my chest pressed against his, I felt all the good intentions of the human heart.

He led me through three songs, a set known as a *tanda*, and that was enough. I had immediately gone from considering tango lessons to needing to know this dance. Marcel suggested a studio for classes and a few private teachers he thought were good.

"Honestly," he said, "it takes a village to make a tango dancer."

Marcel excused himself and disappeared into the crowd. The

shrieking of gulls filled the air, and a thick humidity started to settle over the port. I touched the place where my wedding ring used to be and for an instant wondered where it was. I had grown so used to it—fiddling with it unconsciously at times, at other times acutely aware of it. I had thought that being married meant never having to go through another breakup.

I decided to leave and when I had almost hit the street, the tango music fading to a distant buzz, I turned to watch the group. They were no longer individuals, each with a story, a distinct style; from a distance, they had become a collective noun, part and parcel of the tango community around the world, slipping off on the crisp nights to embrace one another in places as remote as Lapland, or moving in the shadows of the Hagia Sophia in Istanbul, or arriving very, very late, so late that night bleeds into day, at the milongas of Buenos Aires.

The people of Buenos Aires are known as *porteños*, or people of the ports. Currents and winds once ushered in boats full of immigrants from the Mediterranean, carrying remnants of their homeland up the Río de la Plata; black slaves from Africa had been shackled and hauled there; and white slaves, mostly women from Eastern Europe, were tricked into moving there—through marriage proposals and offers of a better life—not knowing until too late that they were to be forced into working the brothels to service this huge influx of men. The tragedy, hardships, and homesickness of these groups overlapped in the south side of the city, where the ships arrived. At these ports the tango was born.

The origins of the word *tango* are debated. Some claim it's African, and in certain dialects it means "closed place" or "reserved ground." Others say it has Latin roots in the word *tangere*, "to touch," and was brought by the Portuguese slave traders. It came to mean the places where African slaves and free blacks gathered to dance. In the ports of Buenos Aires tango grew in popularity, particularly when the Cuban sailors started arriving and introducing a rhythm known as the *habanera*.

By the mid-1800s so many more men than women had arrived that the port brothels overflowed and men danced tango with other men, holding each other at arm's length; they had contact: skin, human warmth, the pulse of another person's heartbeat and the flow of his blood. According to some accounts, though, more than anything they wanted to catch the attention of a woman—and most of the women in the ports were prostitutes. Even prostitutes were in such short supply that they could be picky, charging men for just a dance. If a man danced the tango well enough, she might notice and acquiesce to partner with him. The money he paid her was well worth it: It bought him the touch of a woman's skin, the smell of her hair, the finding of a sort of home, at least for a moment, in the arms of a stranger. In Spanish, the term for the tango embrace is *el abrazo*, which literally means "the hug." This embrace is a hug that doesn't pull too tight, last too long, or promise anything but a song's worth of pleasure. It is neither friendly nor amorous. Much more complex than that, it is a tangle of paradoxes.

Tango is a way to learn through the body, to take one's pain into muscle memory and translate it into something else, something nobler. The contradictions — that comfort could be found among strangers, intimacy felt within a crowd, songs about heartbreak help a person find a way out of it — are embedded in the tango, and it begins and ends with the embrace.

CHAPTER 2

La Salida, The Basic

OUR INSTRUCTOR, DARIO, walked with the pointed toes and erect posture of a ballet dancer. Slight of frame, he had brown hair and lively dark eyes closely set; he wore his shirt collar rakishly flipped up. When he caught his own eyes in the mirror, he lingered in his gaze. But then he snapped his attention back to the students and insisted we stand in a straight line facing the mirror, keeping our feet together, closing our eyes, and focusing on our breathing.

"Feel your feet push into the ground," he said. "Feel the top of your head pulling up to the sky. Now balance your spine so you are aligned over your hips."

To learn the basic steps, we started shifting our weight to one side, then back to the other. We ambled forward, balancing first on one leg, then the other. Once we'd dead-ended at the mirror, fully facing ourselves in ways perhaps more difficult than learning steps, we returned, walking backward, switching weight, pressing down as we stepped.

"Enter the ground," Dario shouted out at us. "Push into the ground. Let your hips fall as you walk." We followed his movements, stepping side to side, back and forth, feet brushing the ground.

He then instructed us to find a partner and form a large circle. We practiced the very basic element of reading our partner's shift in weight and trying to synchronize with it—not embracing yet, but holding each other at arm's length in what's known as a practice hold.

"Men, use the follower's energy. You are not dancing alone. This is not about the ego, it is about your partner," Dario said, standing in the center of our circle. "And followers, don't be passive. He needs to feel your energy to lead."

Between the large windows that opened onto Lafayette Street in Lower Manhattan and the mirrors that flanked us on the other side, the room felt too bright, too exposed for such closeness to another person. This kind of proximity needed the cover of night, but we were revealed in positions of strange intimacy: Our fumbling was just as visible to any bemused passersby as if we'd been dogs caught coupling on the street.

Dario explained that the basic step is the *salida*, which literally means "exit," or "way out," but also has a lesser-known meaning of opening an activity to someone; it can mean an opportunity. He put on a slow tango for us and clapped out the steady four-count beat as we stepped around in a circle, the men walking forward, the women backward. Every few minutes we rotated and changed partners. Each leader had a different feel. The easiest to follow had an unwavering stride, others moved with a slight bounce, and some hesitated, questioning themselves, an insecurity that made it difficult to match their pace. The gaze of my partners made me uneasy. I noted the color of their eyes with a searching usually reserved for the very beginning of a romance: watery blue with charcoal flecks, bark brown around black pupils, murky green with gold irises.

One man held my gaze with an intensity that felt like a challenge, so I stared back into his unflinching amber eyes. Because he looked so much younger than I was—I guessed his age at early or mid-twenties—I interpreted his stare to mean that he was learning not to fear women, rather than as anything that involved me personally. His curly hair was just a shade or two shy of auburn, and he had the complexion of a redhead, with smooth, almost pale peach skin. He was turning out to be the class whiz kid.

"Who knows why we push the ground?" Dario asked the class. "Allen knows the answer."

"To use gravity in assisting our balance."

"*Eso es,*" Dario yelled. "Very good, Allen." Dario started the music again, scrutinizing and correcting us as we walked: "No, push your energy out. Feel it in your center and have it radiate out from you. Push down with your feet. Stretch your head up. Relax your shoulders."

He tapped out the beat as he tried to explain the salida to us. "Feet together. Everybody inhale—always remember to breathe— now, leaders right foot backward. Left foot to the side," he instructed. "Okay, followers stay with them."

The salida followed a basic eight count. Tango music evolved from the 4/4 upbeat, cheerful milonga, which is not only the name of a social dance where people tango but is also a lively type of music and dance related to tango. While some scholars claim the milonga beat is derived from music of the African Congo, others say it is from an ancient Spanish song with Arabic influence, from the Moorish stretch in Andalusia. The Cuban sailors disembarked in Buenos Aires with another dance and music, the *habanera*, which layered another, slower rhythm over the 4/4. The habanera is a derivative of the French *contredanse*, which was brought to Cuba by French plantation owners fleeing the slave rebellion in what is now Haiti. Then opera arrived via Italian immigrants along with Germans toting the bulky, accordionlike bandoneón; the gauchos, or cowboys of the pampas, came to town with their folk music and foot-stomping syncopation. At the ports of Buenos Aires, tango evolved with each group of new arrivals.

Even as the music became more complicated, the lyrics stayed ribald, chronicling sexual conquests, championing dancing skills and unfettered bravado. These early comedic bards had not yet lost their innocence and knew nothing of a broken heart. That would come later, with Carlos Gardel.

We continued walking in a circle, and Dario instructed us.

"Enter the woman," he said, "Enter her space—keep your chests together." He then shouted, "Beautiful Moment. Right now, this is the Be-U-Ti-Ful Moment! This is where your energies mix and you feel tango. Do you feel *tango*?"

Here, you twist at the waist and your chests are still together. During this synchronized torque, your centers of balance, or axes, mingle, and for an instant you share the same intimate universe.

Right then, the leader moved into my space and for a moment our legs moved at different angles, but our chests stayed connected and the effect was sublime. In that quick transition, that moment just before I conceded my axis to the leader, I felt something I had been craving my entire life. I had always thought of tango as a verb, as in "you are tangoing." But Dario described it as a noun, a state of being. It was the most basic of intimacies, and I started to feel tango as a swelling of pleasure that started in my chest and spread through me.

Then my partner and I realigned. Our legs, feet, and chests moved back to parallel and we faced each other once again. The final step of the eight-count basic is the "resolution." Like an exhale, the leader merely slides to the side and the follower does the same. The salida, the beginning and end, the exit and the opportunity, start all over again.

When class ended and we emptied into the hall to change out of our dance shoes, I realized that for one hour I had not felt bad, and it wasn't just the absence of pain. Since finding out about my husband's affair, I had felt like I had been poisoned and was slowly dying. But during class I had experienced a simple happiness, a reprieve from the weight of grief.

I sat down next to a woman named Claire. Her kind, sparkling brown eyes were early indicators of her easy friendliness. While unstrapping my basic black, practical, chunky-heeled dancing shoes, I commented to her, "One lesson a week isn't enough. I'm learning too slowly."

"I want to dance tango every night until I'm exhausted," she said. She tucked one black dance shoe into a cotton bag and then pulled off the other. "Until I just drop."

"I think we're going to be friends," I said.

In fact, Allen, the class whiz, Claire, and I went out to lunch, as we all planned to return to the studio in an hour for the afternoon *practica*. We found a little Vietnamese restaurant in nearby Chinatown, settled around a Formica table, and sipped tea. I still couldn't really eat (my stomach had been a cluster of knots since my husband left, about two weeks earlier), but I stirred the noodles around in the bowl of soup I had ordered and inhaled its steam. Since our common interest was tango, we talked about what attracted us to it.

"I loved that documentary with the kids dancing, *Mad, Hot Ballroom*," Claire said. "So I signed up for ballroom dancing — the classic five. But one night I saw an Argentine tango class, and I went and asked if I could switch and start tango lessons right away. I just knew it was for me."

Allen went next. "I like the music. I think that's what attracted me."

"I'm going to a wedding in Montevideo in December," I volunteered, "and I'm meeting friends in Buenos Aires a week beforehand. I figured it would be more fun if I knew some tango." I didn't tell them the whole truth: that time passed for me in a haze. Constantly lost, I made wrong turns and mistakenly drove over toll bridges with no cash on me. I sat stony faced, pulled to the side while the cops shook their heads and wrote out tickets. I couldn't eat—I rarely felt hungry, and I didn't have the mental capacity to organize myself in a grocery store. I slept on the couch, avoiding our bed, and wore the same jeans and T-shirt almost every day. It was a struggle to pull myself together to work at my computer—and I really needed to work. Between writing out a big check to my divorce lawyer and my monthly expenses having doubled overnight, I had to write and sell articles. But I just couldn't think straight. My world was filled only with bruising memories, raw, bottomless aches, and disbelief that my life had become so uncertain. Every once in a while I called my husband and screamed at him like a person with Tourette's. If I happened to be in public when the impulse hit, other people backed away from me, very slowly.

I was pretty certain that Claire and Allen hadn't told me their full reasons either.

We discussed leading versus following as we mixed lime, fresh mint, and bean sprouts in with our noodles.

"You have more to worry about as a leader," Claire said. "I don't envy them."

"Yeah, but we have to adapt to all the different styles of leaders," I said. "When I was learning salsa, any guy from backwater Venezuela was one hundred percent convinced he was dancing salsa correctly, while the next guy from Puerto Rico had entirely different steps."

"I think the leader gets to interpret more," Allen said. "But he has to be bolder—pay attention to lots of things at once so he doesn't slam his partner into other people. And he has to ask women to dance."

"I run my own interior design business where I make all the decisions, shoulder all the responsibility," Claire said. "I love the thought of not having to be in charge on the dance floor. Following is a relief."

With this, we ventured into territory usually not broached early on among dance pupils—our day jobs.

"I used to teach literature and writing to college students, but I've had enough writing assignments to quit for a while. So I'm home alone at my computer during the day," I said. "I like the social engagement at night."

Allen eventually told us that he worked at a financial institution as a computer technician.

"So do you get irritated at people who call you in a panic, only to find out when you arrive that they forgot to turn on their computers?" I asked him.

"Well, it is nice to finally get a little respect from the brokers," he answered.

We finished the meal and made our way back to the studio,

weaving between the pedestrians and vendors' carts that filled the streets, passing breath mints between us.

Anytime there was a break — in conversation, dance lessons, something to focus on — the dread returned: the feeling like someone had died. I missed my husband. Not the man I was divorcing, but the man I married. The one who met me at the subway station at night and walked me home. Who carried my bike up the stairs for me. Right after our wedding, we had argued over what color linoleum tiles we should put on the kitchen floor. I wanted bright blue, he want a more subdued color. We finally agreed on light green. He laid the tiles and I helped by scraping up the excess glue. He stood and surveyed his work while I was still scrubbing on my hands and knees; either he was admiring his handiwork or my butt in the air, or both. He grabbed me around the waist and we made love on the kitchen floor.

But something changed. His interest in the house ended. He was too tired to go out dancing, and for his out-of-town trips, he departed at all hours of the night. He assured me it was just business.

I thought about the last time my husband and I had made love, the day before I found out about his girlfriend. It was uninspired. His cheeks were unshaven and burned my face. I had trouble falling asleep that night — his body was always hot, but that night it felt toxic, and whenever I bumped against him I jolted awake. I knew something was wrong, but I told myself it was his job.

Then I learned. The next night the computer made an odd mewling, like a barn door opening; he had received an instant message on his e-mail account. I opened it.

"*Loquita, tu es el amor de mi corazon,*" he had written to her. Little crazy one, you are the love of my heart.

"*Tu es un loquito. Te extrano un monton,*" she had written back. You're the little crazy one. I miss you a ton.

At that moment I felt utter calm. I had known something was wrong. Now I knew what.

He was on the road, working, so I called him.

"How did you get my password?" he said.

"That's the least of your concerns. I'm divorcing you," I said. "I'm throwing your shit out and I'm divorcing you."

"Don't throw my stuff out," he said.

I considered this. Since he was out of town, it wouldn't have had much of a dramatic effect. Basically, my neighbors would have had to walk over his clothes for a week. So I agreed to give his things to a friend.

"Don't divorce me," he said. I hung up and called two of my girlfriends who lived in the neighborhood. They came over with bottles of wine. While we emptied them we emptied his clothes from the armoire, pulling shirts and pants from hangers and wadding them into balls. He loved his clothes and took fastidious care of them, washing his tennis shoes by hand once a week, hanging his pants just so. Underwear, socks, and shoes we jumbled and crammed into corners of a huge canvas bag. Once it was full, my friends and I shoved, kicked, and heaved it down the stairs. A neighbor poked his head out of his apartment and asked what was going on.

"Oh, nothing," I said.

He didn't seem convinced, but after looking at the three of us, tipsy and wild-eyed, he knew enough to go back into his apartment.

After the drama subsided, I lay on the couch and watched car lights flicker across the walls of my apartment until I fell asleep. I woke up at sunrise. I couldn't quit thinking about how the past few months with my husband had been a lie. The future I had imagined and hoped for—a child, a house—had been shattered. I sank into an abyss between lies of the past and the pain and disappointment that lay ahead of me. Stretched out on the couch, I thought about what I would do. I had liked being married. I'd felt at peace. I didn't think my husband was my soul mate—I loved him and he was there and willing and I was ready. I thought depth in our relationship would develop over time. I loved the idea of sharing my life with another person. Now I needed a plan, a goal, something to replace this loss and emptiness I felt. My husband and I had planned to attend our friends' wedding. Katherine and Marcus lived in New York but would have their wedding in Uruguay, where Marcus grew up. We were supposed to be flying into Buenos Aires. We had mentioned taking tango lessons. Now alone, I would learn tango and travel there without him. My first stop had been the South Street Seaport, and, convinced I wanted to learn it, I only had three months before Buenos Aires. I made sure that I registered for classes that were followed by a practica, which is a few hours of free dance practice that studios offer their students.

Back at the studio, to prepare for the practica after our first lesson, Dario arranged metal folding chairs in a line against a wall. Afternoon light angled through the tall windows, and dust motes floated in the sun's rays. People sat in the chairs to change their shoes; a few stood in front of the mirrored wall and stretched, while some couples had already taken to the floor and were waiting for the music to begin.

"This is a practica," Dario announced. "Here you can give suggestions and gently correct each other. Never do this at a milonga. In tango, you dance close to your partner, so it's important you are clean and well showered. And leaders, get to know the followers level, where she is and what she's capable of, before trying to kick *ganchos* over her head." He demonstrated, whipping a leg behind him and up into the air. Everyone laughed.

When the music started, Allen and Claire paired up first and I sat and watched. Couples danced in harmony, but also with gestures indicating rebellion, regret, then resolution. They kicked between each other's legs, and sometimes pressed their torsos tightly against each other but then pushed apart; they didn't so much reflect each other as create a rippling back and forth, like underwater motion. Strains from the bandoneón and violin scratched out yearning, and the music swelled around the dancers as they passed through the sunlight that spilled onto the polished wood floor.

It was my turn to practice with Allen, who was a clear, good lead. He held a fearless gaze. I stared right back at him, fighting a slight smile. We worked on our basic, adding the woman's crossover. When he indicated with a twist of his chest, I slid my foot back until it crossed in front of my planted foot. Then both the leader and the follower shift weight. He walked forward as I moved back, and we sidestepped into resolution.

Allen's signal to cross in the basic salida was an obvious, almost dramatic gesture and it was easy to read it. As leaders became more advanced, though, the gesture to basic crossover becomes so subtle as to be almost imperceptible; you have to read the intention itself rather than the gesture. So while I loved the safety of dancing with Allen, I knew I would have to branch out in order to learn all the different ways this lead was signaled. But, for now, we held each other at arm's length until I relinquished him to other followers and took a seat.

"Mi Noche Triste" (My Sad Night), sung by Carlos Gardel, played. *"De noche cuando me acuesto / no puedo cerrar la puerta / porque dejandola abierta / me hago ilusion que volves."* (At night when I go to bed / I can't close the door / because by leaving it open / I make believe that you're coming back.)

Written by Pascual Contursi, this song has no closure to grief, nothing upbeat. It's a lament about lost loves and innocence shattered and an initiation into the world of traitors. In 1917 "Mi Noche Triste" became the first recorded tango, and Gardel became its voice. He sang with conviction, creating an emotional landscape of such volatility that people were known to weep upon hearing him. With this song, the tango changed. It was no longer simply bawdy and full of sexual innuendos. It would no longer be happy.

Next, Dario played a song that seemed to tap directly into my own sadness. The woman's voice was so haunting, it expanded the sense of loss as if it were a space that let you wander around inside, like an empty museum at nighttime. It was "Nefeli's Tango," by the Greek diva Haris Alexiou. I had no idea what she was saying, but from the mournful way she sang, I imagined the lyrics meant something like "My heart has been broken, so I'm going to blind myself and wander in the desert and ponder the misery that is life."

The song filled the studio, and the couples echoed the emotion. Marcel, my acquaintance who had insisted I dance with him at the South Street Seaport, showed up at the practica with his girlfriend, a pretty, slender brunette. At one point he stepped back and let her full weight fall against him. Her free leg extended and swept the empty space; it looked as though she was searching for him with her foot, then trying to find something to grasp onto. The move was so sad, so filled with longing, that I decided I just had to learn it. I watched another couple: The man looked Irish, with ruddy skin, pale blue eyes, a strong jaw and thick neck and was leading an elderly woman around the floor in a tight embrace. They danced quickly, athletically; she swung a leg up, returned it, keeping up with his pace. He wore a bandana around his head, and his casual T-shirt and jeans made him look like a construction worker before a shift.

Marcel interrupted my staring by asking me to dance. He

held me in open embrace, as I needed to watch our feet. Close embrace was still too terrifying, like being instantly blinded.

"Use gravity," Marcel said. "Push into the ground with your legs so I know what foot your weight is on." I tried this and we danced a little, but it must have felt like pushing lead around. "But be light with your upper body," he said.

I sighed and he laughed. "You'll get it."

We practiced the basic, pausing in front of the mirror so I could see my steps.

"Don't anticipate," he said as he walked in a smooth, steady gait. Then Marcel introduced me to the Irish man and pretty much forced him to dance with me.

"I'm a beginner," I explained.

"It's okay," he said.

I tucked my arm around his shoulder and felt his chest press against mine. He smelled vaguely like he was sweating out last night's booze. He pulled me into close embrace and hit a fast pace, stepping on half notes. I let my legs follow his on the pauses. I didn't have time to count, but I was doing it, flaring a leg forward, swinging it backward the way I had seen the other dancers do it. I didn't have time to be scared. My mind cleared and my body just responded. It was exhilarating.

It's said that randomness creates addiction; that if something is reliable, you don't feel as attached to it. That's why gambling is addictive. And why dancing is, too. The social nature of having multiple partners means that sometimes the dance feels stiff and awkward, but the ones that are good feel so good they fuse into your memory, and the possibility of repeating the experience keeps you coming back for more.

When the music stopped, I recognized a young hipster from my neighborhood. Wearing flame-retardant plaid retro slacks and a vintage mustard-yellow shirt, he brought a bit of trendy Brooklyn into the room. He was also a terrific dancer, with original steps and enough confidence to switch up the rhythms. Claire and I stood at the wall and noticed his facial expressions: lips pursed, eyebrows lifted, not smiling, not frowning, just focused.

"It's almost like he's playing a musical instrument," Claire said.

"Only with his feet," I answered.

The Hipster stopped dancing, and he and I chatted about people we knew from our neighborhood. The last time I had seen him, he had just sold his business as a headhunter for tech companies and was going to spend time reading and writing.

"No, never wrote much," he said. "Instead I started dancing tango seven nights a week."

"Every night?" I asked him.

"Yep," he answered. "You'll see."

Then, out of charity, he invited me to dance. But rather than walk the basic, he moved me around the floor quickly and forced me to practice shifting my weight. He'd switch his weight to one side, and I'd have to follow and change my weight to the other foot. It was tough, but I appreciated what he was teaching me. The steps are the easy part in tango; the technique, the embrace, finding the weight shift, keeping balanced on one leg — these are the hard things.

Afterward he suggested I take private lessons. "One private class with Robert T. is worth ten group classes. And if you go to his place in Queens, it's half price."

"How do I find him?" I asked.

"Google 'close embrace,'" he said.

I jotted this down on a piece of paper: Robert T. close embrace.

My friend Kim had invited me to dinner for Rosh Hashanah, the Jewish New Year, at her mother's house, despite the fact I was Catholic. She knew that I needed the New Year to come much sooner than the first of January. When I rang the bell, I remembered the story Kim had told me about her parents' divorce. Her father had left her mother for another woman.

"My mother didn't get out of bed for weeks," Kim had told me. "And my father refused to give me his new phone number. His girlfriend didn't want him to; she was afraid I would tell my mother how to reach them. I was seventeen, with an incapacitated mother, and I couldn't call my father."

When Kim's mother, Sarah, smiled at me that night, I hoped she wouldn't hug me or mention my divorce. I thought that if she touched even my arm or shoulder I would burst into tears. My new awareness of how people suffered from betrayal made me almost unbearably sensitive, and I didn't want my pain mingling with any they might have. It would be too much, or so I thought. We gathered around the table with family members and friends of all different religious denominations. Sarah led the prayers over the food in Hebrew, glancing up when she stated that as this year ends, we approach the new one with hope for a better one. We all dipped apples into honey so that anything in the New Year that was sour would be sweetened.

CHAPTER 3

La Caminita, The Walk

AT FIRST I didn't cry. Then one morning, when I was calculating when my husband's affair had started, I realized it was around the time I had gone back to the Midwest for my grandmother's funeral. She'd had Parkinson's disease for a long time, and as she withered away, my grandfather cared for her. He cooked her soft-boiled eggs and wiped her chin when she ate. He carried her to the toilet, bathed her, placed her back in bed. I had asked him how he was holding up, and he said, "She took good care of me for sixty-five years. I'm going to take care of her now."

When I thought about my grandfather's devotion to my grandmother, when I thought about having to tell him about the breakup of my marriage, that's when I started to cry. And once I started, I couldn't stop. On the subway or at the gym, I'd pretend I was having an allergy attack when tears streamed down my face and I searched my purse for tissues. My eyes were red and puffy all the time, and anything—a couple holding hands, a woman playing with her baby, a rat running by with a hamburger bun—would trigger the waterworks.

Things had not even gotten difficult between my husband and me and he was already cheating. Over and over I had asked him why. His answer: "I don't know. For fun, I guess." I wanted better than that in a partner. For weeks now I'd had a note posted on my computer screen: CALL LAWYER, but somehow I just kept forgetting to go by her office to sign the papers that would start the divorce proceedings. Of course, it wasn't just forgetfulness. I hadn't let him go.

Instead of making an appointment at the lawyer's office, I decided to schedule a private tango lesson. On the way to the session at Robert's, I was crossing the street when my foot hit a crack and I fell. A block away, the light changed, and cars sped toward me. I hesitated, feeling the rough surface under my fingers. I briefly fantasized about being hit by a car. I imagined the impact of the metal grilles and the smell of tires burning on asphalt. I welcomed the oblivion that would follow—that this horrible pain would finally be over, or that at least the physical pain would eclipse it. But what if I lived? It was the surviving and recuperating that would hurt too much. The wired jaw and broken legs. The hours of physical therapy it would take to learn to walk all over again. I pulled myself up and hurried to the sidewalk and stood there for a moment, feeling the back draft of the cars as they passed by me. Embarrassed by the fall, my ankle slightly sore, I thought about just going home, but I instead I went to my lesson.

Robert's apartment was on the small side for a dance studio, but the sparse furnishings gave it a roomy feel. A crimson curtain was the only splash of color, where everything — the radiator, walls, and trim — had been coated with a thick layer of muddy beige paint. The mirrors set around the perimeter were different sizes and shapes; each reflected a particular angle of the room. It was a little like a somber funhouse. I thought it would feel strange to be in an unfamiliar man's home for my private tango lesson, but Robert was all business.

Speaking with a trace of an Irish accent, he first instructed me to go to the wall and stand about two inches from it. He asked me to lean into it, pressing my ribs against it while keeping my spine straight and connected to my torso. He demonstrated how to press my temple against the wall as if it were resting against my partner's forehead. While trying to find the right tango stance with the cool, simple wall, I thought about how I had awakened that morning filled with dread.

Getting out of bed had been a monumental effort. When I finally did, motivated by my private lesson, I shuffled to the kitchen, made coffee, and shook out a cigarette, castigating myself for smoking as I lit it. Still not wanting to eat, this was my preferred divorce-time breakfast. I mentally reviewed what I had to do that day in order to find where the dread was coming from. Then I realized that it was Friday. I had found the love letter between them on a Friday. I had packed up all his things that same Friday.

A week later, also a Friday, at 2:30 in the morning, someone started calling me. "Private" flashed on my cell phone. I answered, and in my drowsy state assumed it was my husband; in fact, I almost said his name. But no one was at the other end of the line.

When someone dies and no body is recovered, or when a person has gone missing, it's known as ambiguous loss. The effects, including lingering grief and disorientation, can go on longer than with a death you witness, a body you bury. This felt like ambiguous loss. Where is the man I married? The one who wrapped both arms around me, then nestled his head into my hair and whispered "*Te quiero*" before he fell asleep. Who pulled me to him first thing every morning, before he even opened his eyes, as if it were a natural response to waking. The man I was divorcing was my enemy, someone I hated. My body remembered the blunt trauma of going from love to hate so quickly. Even when the pain slipped from my mind, my body remembered to feel bad.

I brought my attention back to my tango stance. There was something soothing about the wall: the steadiness of it, the certainty that it could take my full weight.

Robert didn't dance me around the room, holding me close and showing me steps and flourishes as I had hoped. Rather, as we danced he corrected my every move.

"Your legs need to be straighter. Stop. You put weight on both feet. That can never happen in tango. Your weight is on one foot or the other." He started the music, then after a few moments of dancing, he said, "Stop. Now your weight is on the outside of your foot; it needs to be on the ball." Then I wasn't putting enough pressure on him; next I put too much weight on him. The music went off again because I didn't read the shift of his weight correctly. Music back on, we walked around the room, my mind spinning with all the instructions. The tango walk is simply two people moving together while in the embrace to a basic eight count in the music. The leader can shorten or lengthen his stride, walk slowly or quickly, step on either the melody or the harmony. The follower matches his cadence, tempo, and weight change so that their feet and legs mirror one another. The embrace is how the dancers initially connect, but the walk is how they travel together on the dance floor. It's the basis for all other steps to come, and the walk can be one of the first things a tango dancer learns yet one of the hardest things to perfect. Experienced dancers glide over the floor, while beginners just try to hear the music and stay connected to each other.

Next Robert abruptly turned the music off and showed me how to lift my torso by improving my vertical energy. He instructed me to go back against the wall, rest my temple against it, and lean into it. This time it felt a little like a punishment: a tango "time out."

The outside bell rang and Robert buzzed someone in. It was his dance partner, Vanessa, a dark-haired beauty from Berlin. I thought maybe the lesson would be over; instead, when Robert danced with me, Vanessa now corrected my steps.

"Keep time as well, don't just rely on your leader," she said. "Don't lose your axis. You're stepping with it."

Robert chimed in, "Relax your joints but keep your muscles engaged."

Vanessa added, "Feel your back connect to your fingertips. You should feel the floor through your foot that's planted *and* through his shoulder. That's how connected you are in close embrace."

Robert tried to keep me leaning away and embracing him as if in an avuncular hug.

He grabbed a sheet of white paper from his desk.

"Think of this as a check for a million dollars," he said. "If we can keep this between our bellies, without letting it drop, then you get to keep that million dollars."

We walked belly to belly, but soon my million floated to the floor.

I danced with Vanessa next. Robert ran a belt through the loops of Vanessa's jeans and then mine, attaching us at the hips so that I wouldn't stick my butt out and would keep my body aligned. We stepped around the room, forehead to forehead, and Robert heckled, "Wow, if I had a video camera, I could make some money with this on the Internet."

Women usually feel too light and too unsteady as a lead—even if they are good, there's something missing. There's also the breast problem; with two women you have to wedge your breasts around each other's like fitting together Lego building blocks. With men, there's a solidness, and if a connection happens, you feel the mingling that comes from the animus-anima energy. But Vanessa felt good to dance with; she walked with certainty and had a lovely energy, sort of sweet and calming. We walked around the apartment.

"When there's a hesitation in the music, think of it as driving through a yellow light when you notice a cop," Robert said. "You pause but keep going."

And then it occurred to me: the transition. The step is actually a transition. It's not just about pressing into the floor or matching the leader's step. It's about the axis — each person's center of gravity is always maintained, and the transition as you switch weight is only a matter of staying on your axis. This centrifugal force is the crucial constant.

That afternoon felt like a breakthrough. I offered to pay them more, since I'd had two private teachers, but Robert refused, splitting the cash with Vanessa. I had a moment of appreciation for their lifestyle. I knew Robert's life hadn't always been like this. The previous week, after a group class, I had mentioned to a student that I started dancing tango because of my divorce.

"That's why lots of people start," she said. "That's how Robert started dancing tango."

The next morning I made a decision. I would finish the paperwork and take it to my lawyer. I fished a pair of brown shoes out of my closet. Although old, they looked okay, or at least inconspicuous: shiny brown leather shoes, almost loafer style but with rounded toes and thick heels. They had served me well for walking in the city. I'm a minimalist when it comes to shoes; I rarely had more than two pairs I liked to wear in any season, but my black pair needed the heels repaired and my oxblood boots didn't work with my outfit. I had planned on buying new shoes when I took my trip to Argentina; the country had a reputation for producing nice leather shoes, and the dollar was strong there. I took the subway into Manhattan, trying to keep my sniffling inconspicuous, trying not to think about the task at hand so I wouldn't weep in public. Instead I read the subway advertisements: the benefits of fruit facial peels; sexually transmitted disease public-service announcements; budget divorce lawyers advertised in bold black-and-white ads.

As I arrived outside my lawyer's building in mid-Manhattan, I noticed white Styrofoam-type particles coming out of my shoes. The right heel had cracked, as had the left sole. I entered the building, stepping as lightly as possible, but from the corner of my eye I saw the little white particles scattering around me with each step. My poor old shoes were bleeding to death! Fortunately, nobody looked down or seemed to notice, so I signed in, thanked the security guard, slapped on my nametag, and went upstairs to talk with my lawyer.

While I was signing the papers, my thoughts were mostly on my disintegrating shoes.

"Do you know of any good shoe stores nearby?" I asked.

My lawyer shook her head and said, "I don't shop around here."

I hit the street and headed south. I figured I'd drop into any shoe stores on the way, but my primary destination was Macy's, as they had an entire floor of shoes. En route, pieces of my shoes started falling off in clumps. Soon I was down to just half a heel on the right shoe, and the crack in the left sole had expanded into a crevasse. I tried to walk steadily and not attract attention to them.

By the time I reached the department store, the right heel had flaked off entirely, and the left heel now began a rapid disintegration. I limped around the sale racks, looking for practical shoes. The only person who noticed the state of my feet was a little old lady who wrinkled her face in disgust. It was the sort of expression generally aimed at people in New York City who are urinating in public. I sat down to try on some sale shoes, finally slipping off my dying ones, and the soles and leather separated. They looked like flayed animals. The salesman averted his eyes when he brought me shoes to try on. Since nobody else seemed to think this was funny, I called a girlfriend.

"The timing is amazing," she said. "You have to buy something fabulous to replace them."

She was right. In my stocking feet I strode past the sale racks to the Coach section of the store. There I put on a pair of dark chocolate brown suede clogs, lined with faux fur and with brown leather and brass studs covering the heels. They were impractical, expensive, and perversely beautiful. As the woman rang the sale up, I told her that I didn't need the box. Though my new clogs were noisy and a little difficult to walk in, I felt good about swapping them for the old brown loafers.

Encouraged by my new shoes and by setting the divorce in motion, I decided to start throwing out my old stuff the next day. Clothes and shoes I no longer wore, I packed into bags and took to the Salvation Army. I hauled boxes of books that didn't interest me out of my bedroom and set them in the hallway near my front door to take to a used-book store. I emptied an enormous file cabinet that had been in the corner of our bedroom, then disassembled it and took it outside drawer by drawer and left it on the curb. Pictures of our life together — the wedding, trips to seashores and holidays with families, fixing up our apartment together — I put into albums. One for me to tuck away deep in a closet, and another for him — to give him one day in hopes he'd regret his betrayal. I started rearranging the pictures on my walls, but then I took down most of them, leaving the walls bare. As if that would erase memories.

Later I headed into Manhattan to a tango practica, where I sat down next to Claire, and right away we started commenting on the dancers.

"That guy looks like he'd rather be dancing alone," I said, nodding toward a man who syncopated his steps with little stomps, each one seeming to signify impatience with his partner and an effort to prove he was a superior dancer.

"Yeah, the woman just happens to be there," Claire said. "Almost an inconvenience."

Allen, joining us, agreed. "He hasn't let go of ego yet." He shook his head as he watched the guy march around, oblivious to his partner. He and I slipped onto the floor, finding a space among the couples weaving a line of dance.

Followers usually walk backward. Sometimes the leader's steps are short and shallow, at other times they're long and sweeping, depending on his interpretation of the music. Or you might start walking and then the leader pulls you into a rock step, back and forth, back and forth. This often means he's stuck behind other dancers and can't go forward. But sometimes it's just a hesitation or a syncopation in the walk. When we hesitated, I could feel my ankle throb from my fall the day before, and despair would start to creep in. I could hold it at bay by dancing.

I partnered with an elderly man who had graying hair and was wearing a blue cardigan sweater; and then a slight man with closely cropped hair; next, a tall man who was so thin his veins webbed his forearms like road maps. They could have been anyone you sat next to on the subway or stood behind at the grocery store. But they were right there and I needed this anonymous closeness, the comfort of a stranger's touch. I wanted to cling to these men the way a drowning person would to a life raft, to be comforted, so their warmth would stop the throbbing of my strained ankle, the dead weight in my heart, and the sickness in my stomach.

When you feel a connection with another person, the dance is never bad. Sometimes, though, it can feel bad. There's the man with viscous hair gel; the really short man who doesn't dance with petite women and gets his face suspiciously close to your breasts (I dubbed this type the breast nester); and the man whose sweater smells like the stuff the school janitors sprinkle over vomit. (How the hell did he get that scent on a sweater?) Worst of all are the men who take advantage of a beginner's insecurity, blaming their partners for their own mistakes. But the connection, the "tango" feeling, is almost always good.

"I love this," Claire said during a break.

"Yeah, I had a rough day, but this has made it better," I told her.

"What happened?"

"Had to see my divorce lawyer," I told her.

We both looked straight ahead. Two advanced dancers were practicing *ganchos*, or hooks; he bent his knee, she swung her leg through it with a quick kick. He spun, thrust a lower leg through hers; they stepped, flicked again.

"I'm sorry," she said. "Do you mind my asking what happened?"

"He was cheating," I said.

"How long ago did you find out?" she asked.

"Not long," I said. "I started tango right then. Maybe a month ago."

Then she told me that her boyfriend had been cheating on her for two years before she found out. "I didn't want to break up," she said. " I asked him to just not bring anyone to our home. The place I worked so hard to make nice for the two of us. I guess I told him exactly how to end things with me for good. He started bringing them home. It finally forced me to leave."

We watched couples tango by, many of the women with their eyes closed and a dreamy look on their faces while the men navigated the dance floor. The song "Que Te Importa Que Te Llore" (You Don't Care that I'm Crying) played and we stood quietly, absorbing the music, noticing the way the emotional language of dancers changed with the tempo. The song ended with the line "*Si no puede ser aquel ayer de la ilusion / dejame así, llorando nuestro amor.*" (If I cannot have the illusions of yesterday, / then leave me to cry for our love.)

"You're learning how to trust again," I said to her. "That's why you needed the Argentine tango."

Just before I left, I danced with Marcel. The classic "La Noche Que Te Fuiste" (The Night You Left), rolled out a steady, clear beat. When the violins started their crescendos, he pulled me to his chest, his right leg lined up alongside my left, and we walked. I stretched my legs back, matching his stride. Chest to chest, legs mirroring each other, I felt his energy solidly against me; the connection formed between us, warmth washed through me, and I could have walked to Massachusetts like that. Marcel quietly sang along, "*Mis sueños y mi juventud cayeron muertos con tu adios.*" (My dreams and my youth fell dead with your goodbye.) Then, at a slight pause in the rhythm, Marcel stopped me and stepped backward, still holding me to him but pulling me so I had to put weight against him.

"You can lean on me right now," he said. "Put all your weight on me. I'm not going to let you fall."

I allowed him to pull me off my axis and hesitantly rested against him, my rib cage up, my neck and head reaching vertically, my back and legs perfectly straight, abdominals engaged and feet pressing into the ground. I hung on to him and, despite the rigor of the position, let myself relax. I breathed and felt my shoulder against his and the firmness of his foot pressing against the floor. With another inhalation I felt his ribs against mine, his warm, sweet breath on my neck. Then my full weight finally hinged on him and he pulled me even closer.

"That's it, perfect," he said. We stayed there for a moment and the tango singer belted out, "*La noche que te fuiste, se fue mi corazon.*" (The night you left, so did my heart.)

Then Marcel shifted his balance, pushed me back onto my axis, and we began to walk together.

CHAPTER 4

El Ocho, The Figure Eight

"Be-YU-Ti-Ful Moment!" Dario yelled out each time we pivoted. He had created his own style of vocabulary, a sort of fusion of basic English terms spiced with his Argentine accent. One of his favorite terms was "Be-yu-ti-ful Moment," which he emphasized in a variety of ways. He shouted this now, as we kept our feet planted but twisted at the waist, keeping our chests aligned with our partners'. Then the leader steps back while turning his shoulders, indicating to the follower to step to his side. She does this, pivots, and then steps back in front of him. This move is the essence of the *ocho*, or figure eight. The term comes from a time when women danced in long skirts and kept their legs covered; the quality of their step was evaluated by the figure eight their hem left in the dirt.

I tried to forget the nastiness of my week so far and concentrate on these beautiful moments in class. I had visited my divorce lawyer and was told the bleak conditions of divorce in the state of New York. The clean and easy "irreconcilable differences" cannot be used. You can divorce someone in New York for cruel and inhumane treatment, abandonment for one or more years, imprisonment for three or more years, or adultery. The only other ways are one year of living apart under a separation judgment granted by a court or under a separation agreement signed by the parties.

I had told my lawyer, "Adultery. I can prove it. The idiot's e-mail is on my computer."

"It's not that easy," she explained. "A third party has to witness it. The actual *act* of adultery."

"Oh, like a private detective snooping with a telephoto lens," I said.

"Even then, adultery is actually a crime in New York, so nobody admits to it," she said. "This is a remnant from the old days. It was the only way you could get a divorce, so some desperate people staged scenes of them in bed with someone besides their spouse and had it photographed to get out of a marriage. Just forget about using that one. There is a bit of a loophole, though . . ."

She told me that if we had not had physical contact in a year, then I could claim abandonment. If not, we'd have to live separately but stay married for a year. I thought about all the yelling into the phone, the clumsy, outraged text messages we sent back and forth. The phone company had called me to see if I'd like to change my plan to include unlimited texting: We had sent more than three hundred text messages to each other in a week. My ineptness in tapping out words on my tiny cell phone reduced me to sending him one- or two-word messages. "Why lie?" I asked. "I didn't want to hurt you," he texted back. "Didn't work," I wrote. "I'm sorry," he wrote. I couldn't stand calling anymore because I once thought that I heard the woman's voice in the background and I wanted to hurt her, in a twenty-five-years-to-life sort of way. I couldn't live like this for an entire year.

"Okay, where do I sign to say we haven't had sex for a year?" I asked. That lie was worth untangling my life from his and moving on.

My lawyer instructed me not to call my husband during the proceedings. "You want him to think we're on his side," she said. "Call me and vent all your anger. We keep a really long tape rolling on the answering machine at night, so you can talk into the early hours about all the things he did wrong."

"That's how you start every day?" I asked. "Listening to those tapes? That must be kind of interesting. Maybe you should do a one-woman play about it."

"No," she said, shaking her head. "It's just ugly. Good people behave very badly during these times."

I decided then that I wasn't going to let this divorce define my life. I wasn't going to be bitter. Tango could help me do this. Pivoting past the leader's open chest in the ocho class, I kept this in mind. I would learn the ocho as a lesson to make peace with men, to find balance.

Because the follower has a moment of autonomy during her

pivot, she has the opportunity to add embellishments and show her personality. She can kick a leg back in the air, tap her toe, drag a foot on the ground, but she's still not independent — she still has to respect the dynamics of the "us," the partnership.

The origins of the ocho have been traced to Africa. In his book *Tango: The Art History of Love*, Robert Farris Thompson wrote of the tango's African roots. He claims the ocho evolved from a figure-eight dance pattern in the Congo they called *zinga ngodi*, which literally means "enlacing two circles." He writes that "dancing two circles represents 'two ways of seeing.'" He believes the ocho is similar to this Kongo emblem of balance.

"The women of Argentina are strong," Dario said. "They are not waiting for the man. This is a struggle, they defend their territory. It is a give and take."

He had us partner up and stand in our practice circle.

My first partner was a good-natured senior citizen with a ring of wispy white hair around his shiny pink skull. The bridge of his nose came to my shoulder, and though our height disparity may have contributed to the awkwardness, he also didn't seem to know the basic.

"I've been taking lessons for two years," he told me. "I just have a hard time remembering the steps."

"Switch partners," Dario yelled. "And remember to respect the beautiful moment."

More women than men had shown up for class, as usual, so we staggered ourselves between leaders and danced the step alone until we rotated.

"In Spanish the lead is called *la marca*, or the mark," Dario explained to the class. "It is less macho than your word 'lead.' It is a signal, an invitation." He took a student and demonstrated, opening his chest so she could pass. "You don't push her with your hand; instead you invite her with your chest. Okay, change partners and practice."

As for my next leader, it seemed quite possible that this was his first attempt to dance in his entire life. He didn't seem to hear the music but blustered along in ungainly steps. At times, for no apparent reason, he would stop dead in his tracks as if listening to a distant call. Dancing with him was worse than having no partner, and this made me despair—not just about the class, but about my prospects in general. I was returning in my late thirties to the masses of single women in New York City. This was a man's market: Depressing statistics churned out by magazines stated that there were at least 3.5 single women for every single man in the metro area. The imbalance was even worse in the city proper. Some articles blamed this on the plethora of liberal arts colleges on the East Coast; there were more women than men attending them, and the women especially migrated to the big city. Every year a fresh crop of beautiful, slim, well-educated women moved to New York City for jobs. It was grim for those of us who had been there awhile and had suffered through breakups and divorces. We were like the old fish that had hooks and scrapes on them, still circling the farmer's pond. I didn't want to start all over again. Not in my love life or in my dancing.

After I had finished college in the Midwest, I had moved to

Alaska. I spent several years working there and traveling most winters. Then I moved to New York City for graduate school. I had expected to miss the smell and roar of the Pacific Ocean. I had taken picture after picture of the sandhill cranes that gathered near my cabin every spring, and I would never forget the feeling of walking through the wildflowers that grew taller than my head by late summer. These things I expected to miss, but once I was in New York, I found that I also longed for the social interaction of the small town I had left. In Alaska I had once locked my keys in my truck and so many people came out to help—challenging each other and placing bets on who would unlock it the fastest—that it had started to resemble a block party. Here, I was on my own. Another contrast to Alaska was the daunting challenge of meeting men in the anonymous swarm of the city. So after a few years of trying to figure out how people met here, I signed up for a salsa dancing class, hoping at least to find a sort of community.

At Angel Navarro's Mambo Unico I stood behind the other dancers, concentrating on the instructor's feet and counting to myself, "One, two, three, pause, five six, seven, pause." Trying to move my hips and shoulders at the same time made me look like I had some sort of nerve disorder. I still don't know how I stuck with the classes. I suppose the encouragement of the other students and the handsome brown-eyed Latino partners in the classes kept me going. I endured the awkwardness because I believed, or in some way knew, that learning to dance would be worth all that.

The first six months proved humiliating. Nervous, I could barely keep up with the basic steps, and you can forget about moving two body parts at the same time. I attended Saturday afternoon styling classes to learn body rolls and how to shimmy my shoulders and rotate my hips. I started to become more comfortable with following. The difficulty of following is often more psychological than physical. Women of my generation were taught to fend for themselves and to be independent. It takes a while to relax and realize that if a leader respects his responsibility, it can be a very good experience for a follower.

I learned to step on the beat, or on the off-beat if I wanted to, and to spot myself on turns. Then I started going out. At the dance socials, the floor became so crowded with whirling couples that heads banged and ankles and feet became bruised and bloodied by the stiletto heels flashing on the dance floor. But no one slowed down or stopped. Pure exhilaration emanated from the crowd around me — nobody held back while the trumpets and drums called out their irresistible rhythms. The dancers, drenched with sweat, didn't stop until the music ended. We shimmied and swiveled until our hearts raced and our hair matted. The remnants of my sexually repressed Catholic upbringing were mocked and trampled. I realized that this is how life should be lived.

I met my Cuban husband through salsa dancing. He was a perfect lead. Gentle yet in control. He had an excellent sense of rhythm; he kept the beat and wasn't boring. He transitioned from stepping to turn patterns in response to the music. He maintained a polite distance, and at first it was just about the dancing. Then it became a conversation: humorous, amorous, bold, then timid, expressed with our hips, shoulders, and feet.

A salsa band played at our wedding. The claves, drums, and trumpets played songs of seduction and betrayal, yearning and love and disappointment, but most of all, the music spoke of joy. Salsa taught me about seduction—both the wonderful and the dangerous elements of it. There was something more profound to be learned about relationships from the tango.

For me to feel better, I needed to be physical. This was my form of prayer. When I was stressed out or upset in Alaska, I hiked up mountains or kayaked rocky shorelines. Exhaustion always brought me peace, and the natural beauty offered transcendence. In the Bible many dramatic events happen in nature: Moses receives the commandments on a mountaintop; Jesus spends forty days in the desert being tempted by Satan; John the Baptist dunks people in the river to baptize them. In Ancient Greek times women danced ecstatically over mountainsides and through forests, following Dionysus—that is how they found catharsis and renewal. How had humanity shifted so drastically that we expected children to sit in little confessionals trying to remember how many times they lied or cussed? I had been taught this Catholic version of catharsis. It just didn't work for me. How did the body become disconnected from the spiritual self?

In New York it was too hard to make it into wilderness. I had tried and ended up trekking along highways for hours just to get to a trailhead. I attended a small, liberal Episcopalian church, but really it was dancing that filled my spiritual need. Something about music brought wilderness to the city so that I could experience it as a form of prayer. Cultures around the world have danced to communicate with their god or gods. The Hopis danced on mesas as a prayer for rain. The Athabascans danced on hillsides in Alaska, asking the caribou to come. Buddhist monks in Tibet danced to ward off the devil, and in Africa men danced to train for battle, to entice and distract their enemies, to find a mate, to celebrate, and to mourn. It's commonly said that *mambo* once meant "talking with the gods." So the dance floor became the place where I looked for connection and transcendence.

I had put my time into learning salsa, yet now I wanted to be good instantly at tango. I swore to do better each time I made a mistake. I pledged to myself to take more classes, practice the tango walk at home with a book on my head, hold a glass of water in my hand and move my legs to learn to isolate my body parts. I concentrated and tried to balance, relax, stay on my axis, push into the floor. My mind was in a jumble with so many instructions. The dancing didn't tire me, but the persistent disappointment in myself did.

After class some of the more advanced women dancers congregated in the hallways. I spotted Marcel's girlfriend, Angela, and chatted with her about my impatience.

"Six months," she told me. "We were incredibly frustrated for the first six months."

"It's hard, because you have to go to practicas," I said. "But if you're a bad dance partner, some of the leaders won't ask you to dance again. As in, ever again in your whole life."

"Even when you improve," a woman interjected. "The woman always blames herself. And the man always blames her, too."

Several other women laughed and nodded in agreement.

I stepped into the room where the practica had just started and watched Allen leading a fairly advanced dancer around the floor. It couldn't be easy for men, either. Earlier, during class, Dario had asked, "When the woman doesn't know to go into a forward ocho, whose fault is it?"

No one answered, so he called on Allen.

"It's always the leader's fault," Allen had responded, and we all laughed.

"Brown-noser," I whispered to him.

"Very good, Allen," Dario said.

Going to the practicas after lessons was critical for improvement, but they could be oh so painful for a beginner. At the practica that afternoon, I sat on the metal folding chair and pretended I didn't notice when men avoided making eye contact with me as they whisked by and asked other women to dance; once, Irish Guy neared and my spirits rose, only to watch him lean over and invite the woman sitting next to me to dance. The term for women who aren't asked to dance and who sit all night is *la planchadora*—literally, "the ironer."

Typically, you danced a tanda of three to five songs with one partner. Then a short interlude of nontango music played—a *cortina*—and you found a new partner. Unless the experience was particularly bad, then usually one person—whoever suffered the most—excused him- or herself. While *milonga* is a term for a social gathering where people dance tango, it's also a faster, more upbeat song and dance than the tango. It's thought to be a precursor to tango, but dancers learn it after they know the tango. While the milonga played, a very tall, thin man with brittle blond hair extended his hand to me.

"I don't know how to dance a milonga," I explained.

He insisted.

Did he think I was being modest, claiming I couldn't dance, in order to blow him away on the dance floor? We don't live in that kind of culture: I remembered a Chinese student in my freshman writing class. One day she told me she had just interviewed for a job in the school's math lab. When the interviewer asked her if she was good at math, she answered, "No, I'm very bad." In China, where humility is the custom, this means, "I'm excellent at math." I laughed, then explained our way of promoting ourselves. I suggested that she go back and tell the interviewer that she was indeed good at math. This made her so uncomfortable that I proposed she at least go tell them about the Chinese custom as she had told me. They hired her.

The blond guy wasn't Chinese, so "I don't know how to milonga" should have been straightforward. But he didn't slow down, make his lead clear, or release me into open embrace. He kept me pulled tightly to him and slung me around like a stuffed animal in a dog's jaw. After one song of mutual misery, he strode off and not only never made eye contact with me again but quickened his pace, darting by whenever he saw me.

I wanted to follow him, arguing, "I told you I didn't know how to milonga." But I never did; I just avoided eye contact, too. The Irish man I had danced with after my first class not only avoided my glance but also turned his entire head in a different direction whenever he caught sight of me. At him, I wanted to shout, "You can say hello. I won't make you dance with me."

Another man, with a rigid, erect carriage and straight black hair that brushed his shoulders, invited me to tango at one practica. I explained that I was a beginner, which was both an apology and an explanation. He took it on himself to correct my every move.

"Lean back more, I need to feel the pressure of your back against my hand," he said. "Stand straighter," he demanded. "Walk smoother. Your neck should be elongated." His lead was so subtle and hard to decipher and his criticisms so rapid-fire that I thought for sure he'd abandon dancing with me after the first song; in fact, I hoped he would. Instead, he kept on.

"Your hips are moving," he said. "This is tango, not salsa." At the end of the next song, when we broke apart, I rocked on my feet, shook out my arms and torso, and he corrected me, "This is an elegant dance. We do not shake ourselves in tango."

Enough. I excused myself and got a drink of water. I felt sorry for this man; if he thought withering criticism was teaching, he must not have had an easy life.

Later he apologized. "I'm sorry, I'm just eager for you to improve so I can dance with you."

I nodded as if I accepted the apology. But I never danced with him again. He never asked.

There is still gender bias when it comes to who asks whom to dance. Women can ask men to dance, but more often than not, men do the asking. It's kind of like dating. While most women, in theory, aren't against asking a man on a date, they tend to wait for him to ask. I've talked about this with students in my writing classes. While the guys said that they would like to be asked out (I'm sure they are assuming they would be asked out by girls they like, not girls they don't find attractive), the young women said that they use subtler means of attracting a guy. There's eye contact, flirting, making yourself available. So it isn't total passivity on the part of the female—she smiles, she laughs at his jokes, when he asks about her plans she makes herself available, she tells a friend that she's interested. Rarely, though, do women do the asking.

Especially as a beginning dancer, I didn't want to ask a guy to dance who didn't want to dance with me, and so I waited. Thankfully a few men from my class now trickled in to this practica. Allen was a steady favorite. We stood on the shiny tongue-and-groove dance floor and moved into our salida. Soon he stepped back and turned his chest to the side, indicating for me to pass in a forward ocho; when I pivoted to return in front of him, he had his leg blocking me. I loved this. I could step over him matter-of-factly (or trip, if totally taken off guard and moving too quickly), or take my time and caress his ankle with my foot, a flirtatious embellishment known as a *castigada*, or "punishment." During dramatic moments in the music, when crescendos are rising, some followers slowly drag their leg up the man's and then bring it back to their own leg, caress it as well, then step over him. I chose to linger for a moment, with a short, brief rub on his ankle before stepping over his leg.

After the song ended, Allen said he had to leave early. He acted a little sheepish and finally admitted he had a date.

"Don't you dare mention this to Dario," he said.

I chuckled, imagining Dario giving him tango-based dating advice.

"Where did you meet her?" I asked.

"Internet," he said.

"Anything you learned from tango that can be applied?" I asked.

"Sometimes there's chemistry and sometimes there's just not," he said, as he laced up his street shoes.

Allen, Claire, and I had discussed this mystery of chemistry. Allen insisted it was just that: "Literally, it's phenylethylamine. PEA," he said. "It's like a potent amphetamine and dopamine drug cocktail. When another person stimulates this in you, it overrides any good judgment."

"I think it's a thing of the spirit," Claire had argued. "You just know, without even having to talk, that you're compatible."

"I would argue for the senses," I said. "It's a combination—his scent, the sound of his voice, how his skin feels when he touches you."

Allen left for his date and then Marcel asked me to dance.

"Hi, gorgeous," he said. "Will you do me the honor?"

As we danced, he offered suggestions: "Resist a little more.

Don't take your feet off the ground when I turn." "Okay, perfect. Does that feel okay to you?" Sometimes he'd align me in front of him. "I'm looking for your heart," he said. And then he pressed his chest against mine. One time he stopped and said, "You're holding back. What do I need to do?"

"I guess I don't want to make a mistake," I said.

"You know I don't give a damn if you make a mistake," Marcel answered.

Ahhh, Marcel!

After dancing with Marcel, I sat on the metal folding chair and noticed a tall, handsome man I hadn't seen before. When he danced, he took up the floor, heading toward the center of it, laughing with his partner as he made up new steps. Later, I saw him up close and noticed his stunning cornflower blue eyes and sharp cheekbones; when he asked me to dance, I mumbled something about being a beginner.

"It's okay," he said.

"No, I really mean it," I answered. "I just started."

He dragged me through a few steps and, though I thought I was following okay, after three songs, he frantically scanned the room for another dance partner. But tonight, for some mysterious reason, few women had shown up for the practica. As he swiveled his head and saw me looking at him, I shrugged and said, "Sorry, looks like I'm the only available woman."

He laughed, I laughed, and we danced some more together until we started chatting.

"I've been dancing almost two years," he told me. "Okay, relax your foot right there on the floor and let me just drag it over with mine."

He slid my foot a few feet away, I shifted my weight over to it, and we stepped to the side basic.

"Why did you start tango?" I asked.

"I'm a modern dancer, but when I was in Buenos Aires I met this whole tango community and it felt like a family," he said. "Now I'm making a film about gay tango in Buenos Aires."

Handsome and friendly. Of course he was gay!

"A documentary or feature?" I asked.

"A feature," he said. The practica ended, so we stopped dancing and stepped into the hallway to talk about his film. "I have the trailer shot and I'm using it to try and raise funds to make the rest of the film," he said. "But I really have to work on the script."

"I'm a writer," I told him. "I could take a look at it."

"That would be great," he said.

As I punched his name, Peter, along with his number, into my cell phone, we noticed that students from a performance workshop had entered a dance room and were standing at attention, ready to rehearse a routine that Dario had choreographed. Dario had studied ballet before tango, and he incorporated this into his creations. A few pirouettelike turns happened between the ochos, then a pas de deux bled into a standard tango; then the dancers extended their legs behind their bodies, a hybrid of the ballet arabesque and the tango *boleo*. Dario's vision might have been pushing the tradition of tango, but in France, some claim the ballet primed the masses for the tango.

The Parisians, those cosmopolitan trendsetters, with their penchant for the sensual, made tango vogue in Europe. The dance was first performed at the Paris World's Fair in 1878, and Argentinean tango musicians went there to record in 1907; but these brief introductions were mere tremors of the quake that was about to hit.

According to British author Artemis Cooper in an essay in the book *Tango!* it was the Ballets Russes under Sergei Diaghilev and the "explosion of talent, sensuality, vibrant music and exotic colour, which left its mark on almost every branch of fashion and the arts." This ballet company created a craving for the exotic, the foreign, and the previously forbidden. By 1913 tango was the favorite pastime of Parisians: tango trains, charity tangos, outdoor tangos, and champagne tangos proliferated. The craze manifested itself most fiercely in the tango teas. In Paris, no hostess would invite friends over for tea without clearing a space and hiring a piano player and dance instructors. In London, society people invited tango teachers to their country homes to facilitate tango teas, and tango became *the* dance at seasonal balls.

In 1915 the Englishwoman Gladys Beattie Crozier published the book *The Tango and How to Do It*. Her slim book is filled with gems on various ways to arrange tango teas in your own home. She advises scheduling the tea between 3:30 and 7:30 and having it on a Saturday so that men can attend. One should choose a room in the house and clear it out—if the dancing room is too small for serving tea, set up small tables in an adjoining room. In the introduction Crozier writes, "Fashions, like waves, sweep over continents. Sometimes it will be a dance, sometimes a food, sometimes a song, sometimes a freak of fashion, sometimes a game; but the year of 1913 might be called 'The Tango Year,' for the dance has provoked more conversation and evoked more clothes and teas and music than anything else."

At one point, publishers in London blamed poor book sales on tango teas; however, they claimed that poetry sales went up in that same period. Maybe dancing tango readies people for poetry? When the craze hit Berlin, one of the city's largest department stores started offering tango teas to draw in shoppers. Tango teas were held in the Prussian parliament, and the king of Denmark sent dispatches to Berlin, asking for the music from the operetta *The Tango Princess* before it had even been performed.

Peter and I went in to watch Dario's workshop. When the students began dancing their second number, Peter leaned over, pointed at the Hipster, and whispered to me, "You think he'd like to dance gay tango with me?"

I laughed and said, "Don't count on it."

"Oh, I bet he would," Peter said.

We got shushed and then slipped out into the hallway. We watched the rest of the performance through the windows, whispering to each other about the men we thought were cute. Along with the Hipster there was the Martial Artist, a man who took up tango because his sensei told him that he was too heavy and needed to find more levity. With dark hair and dark eyes, he was handsome, and he danced and spoke in a measured, deliberate way. He didn't seem to have transformed his gravity, but rather he had translated it into his tango style.

"Maybe I'll cast him, too," Peter said.

We left together and went to a Spanish bar nearby and ordered olives and glasses of Rioja. Peter told me the protagonist in his film was a journalist who goes to Buenos Aires to report a story. His mother has just died; he and his father were always distant. He starts taking tango lessons at a gay guesthouse. From there, the romance and intrigue begin.

The love life of the main character was suspiciously similar to his own and the description of his film dovetailed with personal details of his life, and I learned about the man he had been with in Buenos Aires. "Marco stopped seeing me, stopped returning my calls," Peter said. "I tried to get an explanation, but he said, 'You are leaving, going home, why bother?'"

"Were you leaving?" I asked.

"Yes, but I was coming back," Peter said. "And then he accused me of sleeping with everyone I cast in my film trailer."

"And?" I asked.

"Well, not everyone," he said. "Besides, it was before I met him." Peter had become enmeshed in the gay tango scene, and he confessed that he didn't want to be promiscuous. He swore that finding sex was easy, but he wanted a boyfriend.

I told him about my upcoming trip to my friend's wedding in Montevideo. I was set to spend a week in Buenos Aires beforehand with friends.

"You have to go to the gay milonga," he said. "It's the best in town. And take lessons with Marco."

I added his suggestions to my list, which was starting to grow as I told people about the trip. There existed a network among tango dancers: I found out where to dance, the best places to buy shoes, and which instructors to seek out. Peter and I paid our bill and found our way to the nearest subway, where we parted. It was an odd moment, as if we had just gone on a first could-be-a-new-gay-friend date. He leaned over and gave me a peck on the cheek.

"Are you going to the milonga at the studio this Saturday?" I asked him.

"No, I go to gay two-stepping on Saturdays," he said. "I'm going to start teaching gay tango classes here and I need to go recruit dancers."

"Okay, good luck," I said, and kissed him on the cheek, then went down the steps to the subway tracks. While I waited for the train, I thought about the ocho and how those "beautiful moments" in life, when two people meld into a seamless one, could be so hard earned at times and at other times so natural.

CHAPTER 5

La Milonga Primera, The First Milonga

THE LIVELY DANCE known as milonga requires couples to step in a crisp staccato, marking each beat. Milonga the social gathering takes place anywhere: a park, a port, a dance studio with lights dimmed, a Greek restaurant on a slow night, or an old warehouse. You just need a floor that's more or less level, some music, and dancers.

The official difference between a practica and milonga is that a practica is usually held after class at a dance studio and the dancers can correct each other. During these sessions partners work out steps in preparation for the milonga. At a milonga it's bad manners to give suggestions or introduce a new step in the middle of the floor; although some leaders like to do this, it is wrong, wrong, wrong. But really, the most striking contrast between these two dance gatherings is the way people dress. People frequently dance in jeans and T-shirts at practicas, but at the milongas, especially ones held on Saturday nights, they dress more formally.

I knew I had to start pulling together an outfit and that the look was totally different from salsa clothing, which tended toward tight, casual tank tops and pants with some stretch and give. For tango, women wore dresses and hose. So I rifled through my hosiery drawer and tossed potentials onto my bed. The black, opaque winter-wear tights wouldn't work; my one pair of fishnets had a large hole, and I discovered the other stockings had runs, too. My dresses were just as dismal. An old, too-tight black halter-top sheath was the best I could come up with; when I yanked a loose thread, the entire bust bunched. Limping into my first milonga dressed in ratty hose and a dress with dangling threads, I would not have looked like an Argentinean prostitute with a heart of gold, the prevailing tango fashion for women.

I fingered my wedding dress, the exquisite chenille silk, cut tea length so we could dance salsa at our wedding. I wondered if I should one day hem it up and dye it black or green and use it for tango; this I envisioned when I was doing "my forget-my-husband exercises."

I had bought a self-help book called *How to Mend a Broken Heart*, which I briefly considered reading on the subway to see if people wanted to tell me their stories or would instead move as far away as possible. But I kept it private and read it at home. It included exercises like "The Calm Anchor Technique" and "Return to Sender." In one, the book instructed visualization of only the bad times with your former love. When you get a clear picture, make it go blurry and then bleach it out like an overexposed photograph. Finally, visualize moving down a hallway, away from the present, toward a happy future. The author encouraged readers to make it vivid, in color, and to try not just to see it but to feel it, as well.

I pictured myself in an emerald green cocktail dress, heading to a stone patio and dancing tango with a handsome man who loved me. Sometimes the dress was black, and sometimes the patio had a fountain, but the fantasy varied little—I put my faith in the persistence of this vision. I painted in details: trees rustled in the nighttime breeze and the faint smell of sweet water perfumed the air. This Hollywood version of love, or at least of romance, was silly; I had nothing to lose. Sometimes, when I missed my husband, I closed my eyes and erased, overexposed, deleted, and shredded him.

To prepare for my first milonga, I went to a discount department store in Lower Manhattan and bought hosiery, sheer onyx thigh highs, fishnets, side-floral sheers, and midnight black with zigzag-stiched back seams so I had plenty of options; then I went to the dress department and bumped right into Claire.

"I'm looking for tango clothes, too," she admitted.

We decided we should stick with basic black—a splash of red or gold would draw too much attention to our beginner's fumbling. Forget about my emerald green dress. Also, we agreed to remain with our modest shoes for the time being.

"Yeah, I'm staying low until my balance is more certain," I said. Shoes give away the level of a woman's dancing. Practical black with thick, sturdy heels, sometimes called a "granny shoe" in dance circles, means that you're a beginner. As your dancing improves, the heel gets higher and thinner. You have to upgrade. It's like playing a video game—you take your heels up a level and it keeps getting harder, faster, higher. As you advance, the shoes themselves get flashier too: Silver and rhinestones, red satin, gold lamé on 3½-inch stiletto heels send a signal to potential dance partners: "I dance and you'd better, too."

Claire and I agreed to brave our first milonga together. We also convinced Allen to go so we'd have someone to dance with.

ON A SATURDAY night, clean, pressed, modestly shod, and dressed in somber black, we paid to enter the milonga, and then the three of us stood at the entrance to the dance floor and watched. "When I arrived, these little old ladies were inching their way up the steps," Allen said. "I almost offered to help them. But look at them now." He pointed out a couple of gray-haired women who were working the dance floor in saucy evening dresses and spiky heels.

When tango was in its heyday in New York City, it dictated women's fashion. In a *New York Times* article published in 1913, one fashion writer stated, "Well, call it as we will, this new and accepted kind of dancing influenced all the clothes we wear. Gowns are short because of this fashion. Not too short. Their continued narrowness keeps them from being a nuisance . . . It is a waste of time for any person to say at the present moment that she will not need a certain gown for dancing. No gown is free from such usage. Dancing is now a side attraction to every form of pleasure and exercise. You step a measure while you eat and during many hours when you should be asleep."

In Paris, gowns were created for the tango teas. The "tango frock" was a simple gown with a short skirt that might also have a brief train falling down the back.

At this first milonga, belle époch styles meshed with those of Old World Argentinean prostitutes and street roughs. It was mostly charming, though some outfits were so age inappropriate I had to do double takes, as was the case when I spotted a tiny senior citizen in a faux python bodysuit. Irish Guy was gussied up like a spry pimp in a bright fire-engine-red hat with matching red suit, black vest, and white dress shirt, and he gilded the lily with shiny two-tone black-and-white perforated leather shoes. Martial Artist had a subdued melancholy ruffian look in a black suit, white shirt, and black tie; some men wore rakish hats and ascots; others waxed more elegant in their pinstripe suits and buffed black ballroom-dancing shoes. Hipster wore cotton cargo pants, a retro dress shirt with an oversize collar, and a cotton bandana around his head, presumably to catch the sweat, but it made him look like a Caucasian sushi chef.

I spotted Marcel, looking a little like a maître d' in a crisp white shirt and black pants. But my attention immediately shifted to a woman pressing seventy who wore a miniskirt, thigh-high stockings with tiny black bows on them, and a black corset that thrust her bust forward and her butt out, giving her the semblance of a pigeon. A dapper old man in a black wool vest with a pocket watch asked her to dance.

"Well, this is it, guys," Allen said. "Our new social crowd." We all nodded, smiles spreading across our faces. Then Allen and I embraced, close but still keeping a distance between our stiff bodies. Barely daring to breath, we joined the dancers circling across the floor. We moved into the basic, terrified but dancing, more or less.

Close embrace dancing is also known as salon style. The steps are small and subtle, and couples stay joined together as much as possible. It's said that this form evolved from crowded milongas in Buenos Aires. If you took big steps or made wide turns on your ochos, you could bang ankles or slam into one another. So couples clutched each other and moved in tight circles around the dance floor. After Allen and I had made it through a few tandas, we stood around at the snack table in a side room, pouring wine into plastic cups. Potato chips, popcorn, and crudités had been set out by the event organizer. A photograph of the great singer Carlos Gardel was pinned over the table of uninspired snacks. This all seemed a gesture to make the milonga less pastiche and more authentic, more Buenos Aires. But, actually, tango has long been part of New York City culture.

The craze sweeping Europe hit the United States in 1913. Tango was so popular in New York that theater owners found their tickets sales lagging. Managers started incorporating tango into the shows and hosting dances during intermissions. People preferred tango to dining, and in order for cafés and restaurants to make money, they invented the "cocktail," selling drinks during the dances and stretching out predinner activities.

"The Girl of To-Day," as coined by a *New York Times* writer, was described this way: "Her gowns, her tango teas, her votes for women, her wild exultation in the so-called freedom — all have had an influence upon her. And out of this, or in spite of it, has come a new American type." Many of these "girls" were also suffragists. During this time, Margaret Sanger was teaching women about birth control and Anthony Comstock was nipping at her heels with his Society for the Suppression of Vice.

Leaders of the temperance movement fought for women's right to vote in order to aid their battle against liquor consumption. They figured that if women voted, they would all be against legal alcohol. But when it came to dancing, suffragists and preachers were not allies. The Reverend G. L. Morrill, pastor of The People's Church, preached, "The tango is popular because it is depraved." And then, not mincing words, he added that it is the "dance of death" and "its step in time slides to hell."

Another advocate of prohibition of alcohol also railed against the dance craze. In a sermon delivered at Calvary Baptist Church in 1920, Dr. John Roach Straton warned: "The plea that these dancing masters make that they desire to 'purify the dance' and make it safe, is idle and entirely beside the mark. You cannot make a rattlesnake respectable and reliable. The only thing to do with a rattlesnake is to chop off its head, and the only thing to do with the entire dancing mania, which has done more to corrupt the morals of this age than any other single force, is to destroy it, root and branch."

Dancing not only encouraged women's independence, but it also connected high society to new colonies and developing countries throughout the world. In self-defense, British dancers debated the origins of tango to distance themselves from the "primitive." By studying postures of figures on vases and statues in museums, they determined that the stances and moves of tango came from Greco-Roman times. In fact, they announced, tango was once a war dance of the Ancient Thebans. They knew it came from Argentina but were certain that it couldn't have anything to do with the Indians, the cowboys, and especially the Africans. Still, the backlash from the top of the social hierarchies was fierce.

Queen Mary announced that tango must be banned from any society affairs that she attended. Kaiser Wilhelm officially forbade the tango; officers in the army or navy would be dismissed if they were even seen in places where the tango was danced. The pope weighed in and expressed the official disapproval of the Vatican, and the archbishop of Paris outlawed the dance.

Despite this, the masses continued to dance and the tango flourished. As an editorial writer during that time pointed out, "Tango teas are a symptom of a common complaint, namely— the need for more happiness and more individual expression in life." Tango was popular with older, wealthy women whose husbands worked late or traveled out of town, so New York establishments started hiring accomplished male dancers to entertain them. These young men were designated "gigolos," the most famous being a tall, dark, and handsome immigrant from Italy, Rudolph Valentino, who originally wanted to be a gardener.

Valentino was having a hard time finding work in New York City, so he started dancing professionally. He worked his way from New York to Hollywood as a tango escort and teacher (still hoping to be a landscaper), and then started working as an extra in silent films. He was cast as an Argentinean who danced tango in the movie *The Four Horsemen of the Apocalypse* (1921), which not only made him a star but helped fan the tango craze internationally. This created the fantasy—or stereotype—of the Latin Lover.

I kept hearing that tango was now on the rise around the world. A popular television show, *Dancing with the Stars*, matched famous and quasifamous people with professional dancers. They competed in ballroom and Latin dance. I cringed when I watched the show, though, admittedly, I rarely missed it. Sometimes I had to call Claire and lament, "Dear God, Wayne Newton is dancing something they're calling the tango. It's terrible, but I can't seem to avert my eyes."

"What's a Wayne Newton?" she asked.

"He's a singer, I think," I answered.

Then I'd get upset when the professional dancer gave a completely inaccurate history of the tango. Once, the professional dancer informed millions of viewers that you keep your back straight in tango because that's the way Argentinean cowboys ride horses. I'd yell, "No! You're so wrong," at the television set. It was a highly emotional hour for me. But apparently this show has more and more Americans out there learning the waltz, cha-cha, and tango.

In New York City you could find at least one milonga every night of the week, and this subculture didn't seem to have much influence on the mainstream. At a milonga I attended one night, couples left the dance floor and made their way toward a card table laden with stale cookies and crackers and malleable potato chips; Breast Nester, the man who liked to dance with tall women so he was at eye level with their cleavage, came to the table and helped himself to a saltine and a squirt of wine out of the box. This didn't really feel like a glamorous craze—it was more like a random club.

Allen and I helped ourselves to some snacks.

"Hey, how did your date go the other day?" I asked Allen.

"Really well," he said. "We've gone out once since then and I think we'll see each other again. She's really interesting."

"What's that mean?" I asked.

"You know, it was good. She was interesting." He blushed a little.

"Interesting in a good way, hmm," I said. "So there was chemistry?"

"Yep," he said. And I thought I saw him smile a little. Then he blushed, "At least, I think so," he added.

Allen asked Marcel, who had joined us, about what he did for a living. He wanted to make conversation but almost immediately knew that this was a faux pas. People were here dressed in ersatz clothing to take on a fantasy persona. Claire and I had nicknamed Marcel Ambassador, as he welcomed all the new people to tango, helped women who were learning, dj'd the practices, and greeted everyone warmly by first name. His day job was entirely, utterly, beside the point.

"I work for Verizon," he said. He paused for a moment. "I'm a technician."

After an awkward silence, the conversation turned back to tango. Allen tried to redeem himself by asking Marcel for tango advice, and then the little old ladies found Allen and pulled him out to the dance floor. He disappeared into the crowd. I watched the couples slowly circling, embracing one another. I was grateful for the anonymity. I hated running into people I knew. I wore big sunglasses and took back streets in my neighborhood. But every once in a while I'd hear my name, and some casual acquaintance I hadn't seen in months would be standing there, shoulders squared, ready to greet me.

"How are you?"

"Okay," I'd say. Then I'd adjust my glasses over my red, swollen eyes.

"How's your husband?"

This question — meant to be polite, and normal under most circumstances — felt like a sucker punch. What could I tell them? So I figured it was best to get it over with.

"We're divorcing," I'd say.

The "I'm sorry" was almost always followed by a "why?" And I usually told people that he was having an affair. I needed to make clear that I wasn't at fault; I suppose that made me feel more like a victim than just a failure.

"Well, you look great. Have you lost weight?" they'd say.

"Yeah, thanks. I'm smoking again."

I contemplated sending out a holiday greeting card with an image of my divorce lawyer and me on it, along with a note: "Well, this year held a lot of surprises . . ."

But really, I felt deeply ashamed. When I told my mother, she begged me not to divorce him. She wanted me to call a friend of mine, a priest, and ask him for counsel, believing he'd talk me out of it. My mother, a devout Catholic, considered divorce a sin—and although adultery is also a sin, he committed it, not me. (You learn this sort of logic when you grow up Catholic.) I did speak to my friend the priest, and his response was, "You deserve better." When I told the pastor at my Episcopalian church, he commented, "He's an idiot." But I stopped going to church after that. I couldn't control my sobbing when I was sitting at mass, and when I tried to pray, my thoughts streamed out as foul-mouthed invectives aimed at God. I just bowed out of the whole thing.

I had hoped for my parents—or at least my mother—to be fiercer. But in our society divorce is also failure, and she was ashamed to tell people in the Midwest. She also didn't want me to be single. In her circles, singleness was social doom for a woman.

My parents had married young, in their early twenties. A lifetime together is tough for anyone. There were times when my parents might have divorced if they hadn't had five children, if they hadn't been so Catholic, if my mother hadn't been so terrified of being alone. They stayed together, forming each other over time, the way rivers and rocks form canyons—my mother a high-strung perfectionist, my father a man who can nap anywhere, anytime and whose e-mails are hard to decipher through all the misspellings. I got a bit of both of them—overextended and a lousy speller.

One time in high school I was stood up on a date. I waited and waited, until I finally called his house and one of his brothers said he was out with friends. I was crushed. I didn't want to cry, so instead I got angry and began throwing things around the room, not hard, just pillows against the couch and a tennis ball against the wall. Then I sat down at the bottom of the stairs. Our dog came over and put his head on my knees, and I scratched around his ears and cried anyway.

My mother came downstairs. She had rolled up her hair in large blue plastic curlers and wore a long kimono and her heavy, black-rimmed reading glasses. "Why are you home?" she asked. "You had a date."

"He didn't show up," I said, blowing my nose.

"He stood you up?" she asked. Without pausing for a response, she said it again, as a statement this time, not a question. "He stood you up. That little son of a bitch."

She stormed into the kitchen, where my father was drinking beer and listening to the K.C. Royals game on the radio.

I heard clattering.

"You want to know what I'm doing with the meat cleaver?" she yelled. "I'm going over there and I'm gonna kill the bastard. Don't tell me to calm down."

(My mother will totally deny the meat cleaver, and perhaps I just picture this now to make the story more dramatic. Besides, our cutlery and cooking utensils were usually so dull they wouldn't draw blood. But I remember her as armed and dangerous.)

She appeared in the hallway.

"What's his address?" she yelled at me, holding the cleaver up. "Tell me his address, 'cause I'm going over there and he's gonna be sorry."

She stormed out the front door, her kimono flapping. She got in the station wagon and turned the key, but the engine wouldn't start. She held down the gas pedal and kept cranking. A few curlers had fallen out, and coils of black hair fell around her face. She was so angry that her eyes were flickering behind the thick lenses of her reading glasses. The car started with a roar and she yelled, "Tell me his address."

"Please come back inside, Mom," I said.

Then I started laughing. "It's okay, Mom," I told her. "Please come back inside."

The car engine sputtered for a few moments, but she didn't know which way to go, so she finally turned it off. We went back into the kitchen. My mother put the cleaver away, muttering the whole time, "He was never good enough for you."

My father was frying bacon. There's nothing, he believed, that couldn't be solved with a good night's sleep or a bacon, lettuce, and tomato sandwich.

"Who are the Royals playing?" I asked.

"Milwaukee Brewers," he said.

He sliced tomatoes, washed lettuce, spread mayonnaise on

bread (not evenly, but I was too depleted to point this out to him), and started layering everything. He cut one sandwich in half and placed it in front of me, and then made one for himself. We both sat and ate without speaking as we listened to the ball game on the radio.

When I threw my husband out, my dad called.

"Well, make sure you get plenty of sleep," he said. "How's your diet?"

This infuriated me. I didn't want food or sleep. I wanted my father to go kick my husband's ass, but my dad's not that kind of guy. He's a laid-back, make-the-best-of-a-bad-situation sort of person. My mother didn't get involved at all.

"Tell him that he broke my heart as well," she said.

When I finally fessed up to the man who owned the local bodega, Mohammed, why my husband wasn't coming in anymore, he was shocked.

"Why would a man ever cheat on you?" he asked. "You are one in a hundred women—no, make that a thousand."

Tears started welling up in my eyes. People glanced at me as they bought their toilet paper and cigarettes and shook out change for a lightbulb or a mousetrap. Then they hurried away.

"I don't know why," I said.

"If I see him again, I'll kill him with my bare hands," Mohammed told me. He raised his fists into the air and then slammed them down on the counter.

"Thank you," I replied, and sniffed. "I'd appreciate that."

"You need some baklava," he said, tucking a slice in some wax paper and pushing it toward me. "You're getting too skinny."

In the tango crowd I was a beginner with no past, and that suited me fine. The *tangueros* had chosen to live the metaphor: the intrigues, romances, rejections, and slights were not real. I had no intention of meeting a man dancing tango, and Claire fully rejected the idea. "My ex-boyfriend and I did judo together," she told me. "When we broke up, I felt ostracized from the community. I'm not going to make that mistake by dating someone in tango." But I found a haven here. I didn't have to tell anybody what happened or answer painful questions or listen to commentary. And dancing boosts your spirits. Any exercise that gets your blood pumping lifts your mood. As the heart rate increases, the brain starts to stimulate the neurotransmitters dopamine, serotonin, and norepinephrine, all of which work to shake depression. These feel-bad battlers also encourage your body to create endorphins, which make pain go away and replace it with euphoria. If you do a computer search on these chemical reactions, what frequently pops up is cocaine and heroine addiction. The highs people experience from narcotics come from the release of neurotransmitters. With dancing you add music, socializing, and touching. Human touch, our first language, breaks through our isolation and relaxes us—our pulse slows and muscle tension softens. When civilians, or nondancers, can't quite understand why some people want to dance every night, my explanation is that dance is highly addictive, and tango especially so. Physiologically, dancing tango is kind of like mainlining heroine. Only, you don't rob from family members or nod out in public.

IRISH GUY, WHO usually crossed to the other side of the room when I entered, chatted with me and told me that he had only been dancing for two years.

"But I dance every single night," he said. "By the way, you look nice. Most redheads are too pale for black, but you pull it off."

"The alabaster skin," I said. "Another curse of the Irish."

"Bad skin and bad teeth," he said.

"And bone spurs," I added.

"We have strong livers," he answered.

"Good literature, bad food," I said.

"And a sense of humor," he said. "You want to dance?"

We went onto the floor, and within the first minute, he said, "Oh my God, you have improved."

"Last time I danced with you it was my first day," I explained.

"You were just terrible," he said.

"That was two months and many lessons ago," I said.

"My back hurt afterward," he said.

"Oh, I wasn't that bad," I answered.

This ornery guy could dance. He crossed his legs behind himself, bumping my leg in a displacement as we walked, which I would later learn is called the *sacada*.

"Relax," he said. "Don't move your leg until I touch it." He tried it again. Then on a basic crossover he said: "Slow, you don't have to please me. Do it in your own time."

So I tried to slow down when I crossed my legs on the basic. "Slower," he said.

I dragged a leg across the floor.

"Good," he responded.

When the song ended, I marveled at how my first dance with him had been such a good experience for me and so awful for him.

To enjoy a social dance and make the evening worthwhile, you need only three good dance partners. I missed my new friend Peter that night. With Peter, Allen, and Marcel I felt like I could learn; I could make mistakes and be forgiven. I wasn't so sure that was the case with many other people — if they had a bad experience with me, they would never, ever ask me to dance again. And I hated to think that while I was enjoying myself, my partner was miserable. I remembered when I had asked my husband, through sobs, why he started up with that other woman. Hadn't he been happy?

"It's not like that," he had said.

My eyes started to tear up at the milonga, so I forced myself to stop thinking about my ex-husband. "Visualize," I commanded myself. I erased, shredded, and banished him from my thoughts and tried to picture myself in the emerald dress, making my way down a hallway and into the arms of a handsome man. Unfortunately, the only images that came to mind were of little old men dressed as pimps and gauchos.

At 3 o'clock the milonga came to a close with "La Cump-arsita." That was always the last song—playing anything else would bring bad luck. The story goes that the title comes from a slang term in Buenos Aires, *comparsa*, that means to go to a carnival dressed in costume, usually wearing a mask. In 1920s Paris, when people requested tango they got the song "La Cumparsita," and from there it spread. Gardel crooned the sad lyrics, "the masked parade of endless miseries promenades . . . ," and this became synonymous with tango. Around the world, milongas now end with this song, this sentiment; then coats are donned over formal wear, feet slip out of high heels, aching arches are rubbed for just a moment before stepping into street shoes; people metamorphose back into receptionists and moth-ers and scientists and technicians and schoolteachers and ad-ministrators as they catch trains home in Tokyo, shuffle through snow in Scandinavia, walk into the worn nighttime air of Rome, or follow the flow of the Seine out of the heart of Paris.

Now we, too, spilled out into the streets, hailing cabs and disappearing into New York's subway stations. Allen walked Claire and me to our subway stop. He seemed to have a spring in his step.

"I think the first milonga went well," he said. "Considering."

"I have to improve," Claire sighed.

"It takes time," I said, "though I feel desperate to improve also. I hate apologizing before every dance."

"Every night," Claire said. "I'm going to dance every night."

We reached our subway and parted from Allen.

"See you soon," I told him.

"Tomorrow in class, in fact," he said.

On the way home, my neurotransmitters slowed down. The serotonin and dopamine stopped pulsing and the endorphins subsided, leaving a vacuum that created a crash. This is how the dance addiction gets started. When I got home I lit a cigarette but felt nauseous. I threw it out, along with the rest of the pack. I was done with that. A stomachache hit me and knocked me onto the couch, where I rested for a while. Then I hobbled into the bathroom and drew a hot bath and soaked until the throbbing in my feet stopped and the twisting in my stomach subsided. By the time the water cooled off, I realized that I was hungry, starving, in fact. I craved baklava and bacon.

CHAPTER 6

La Sacada, The Take

I STUDIED GRACIELA. Her pants were rolled up, revealing her long, shapely legs, which were accentuated by sparkling blue stilettos; her obsidian hair was haphazardly pulled off her face with rhinestone-studded clips. She walked around the classroom, snapping her fingers and encouraging us to walk in time to the music: "Remember mus-i-cali-ty," she enunciated. "Breave," Graciela yelled at us in an Argentine accent heavy with Italian intonations. A few people looked around.

"Breathe," someone said.

"You have to breave to feel the music," Graciela said. "You have to feel the music to dance tango. And when you make that connection with your partner, it is a pleasure you will never want to leave."

She told us to pair up, explaining that this was an exercise in trust. To demonstrate, she chose a woman from the group and told her to close her eyes. Then that woman's partner took her by the hand and led her. He walked in circles and bent at the knees. She would get so close to the floor that she could brush it with her fingertips. Then he would turn her in a slow spin.

"Learn to trust," Graciela said. "You are never alone in tango. You must trust your partner."

With my eyes shut I felt a moment of panic, but I loosened my clenched jaw and tried not to think. I concentrated on the music as my partner bent down and I squatted to follow; he put my hand on the dance floor and I felt the grain of the wood, barely discernible under the polish. When we stood up, I sensed the nearness of the wall by an increase in coolness; he put my hand on the smooth surface, and through it I could feel the vibrations of traffic outside. He led me in slow, deliberate circles. Then my partner stopped and turned, and we began walking in a different direction; I started to feel more comfortable and stopped worrying about navigating; I had heard the music, but now I began really listening.

"The tango will change you in ways you can't imagine," Graciela said. "I recently had an actor study with me because he was in a play where his character dies. He wanted to learn the tango so that he could die convincingly."

Surrender is what a follower learns in tango — the dance term is *entregarme*. It's a reflexive verb and means "I surrender myself." So it's not defeat; rather, it's a choice to give over one's will. The follower surrenders herself to the lead, to the music, to the experience. It's remarkably difficult to let go of all sense of control and to trust so completely. Despite all my women's studies classes in college, my strong beliefs in feminism, I knew that I needed this right now. I wasn't going to be able to get through this breakup without it.

I thought about the night last week when my friend Amy had come over to my apartment. She set Brie cheese and bread on my kitchen table and started sautéing chicken breasts. I watched her from my chair, overwhelmed with gratitude. I was going to get to eat and it required no thought or effort on my part.

"This is exactly what I need," I said.

What I didn't add was "how did you know?" Amy's husband of seven years had cheated on her with a woman she had considered her friend. While Amy's father was dying of cancer, her husband had served her with divorce papers and then moved in with his girlfriend.

We cut into the chicken, sipped white wine. This was our communion of sorts; we both knew that, at first, there's really nothing that takes away the pain. It's just a matter of staying alive until you find your way out of the darkness. Until then you dead reckon your way around daily life. People who'd been betrayed — left by a spouse, abandoned by a parent — were my preferred company.

"It's a form of insanity, this horrible feeling, isn't it?" I asked Amy.

"I'm so sorry you have to go through this," she said. "But you can grow from it. Think of this as cleaning house so that true joy can come into your life."

Amy had just become engaged to a wonderful man, Isaac; she called him "the lion heart." He was a native New Yorker, but he wasn't jaded. In fact, he was the kind of man who always crossed the street to carry a neighbor's groceries, patted a dog on the head, or helped a woman take her baby carriage up the subway steps. He adored Amy and was a much better person than her ex-husband would ever be. She was living proof of a happy ending.

But it had taken her a while. Amy told me that you get only a year, during or just after your divorce, to behave badly, sometimes even dangerously. Newspapers and local news stations constantly reported crimes that were acts of passion during breakups and divorces, the homicides by people whose neighbors swear they aren't capable of murder, the attempted suicides, the setting fire to homes. A friend of mine called me constantly when his partner, the mother of his child, left him. One day he sounded a little sheepish.

"I saw her new boyfriend today," he said. "He was riding his bike as I drove by."

"I'm sorry," I told him. "Are you okay."

"I tried to run him over," he told me.

"You can't do that," I said.

"I couldn't help it," he answered. "Fortunately he jumped out of the way in time."

While I searched the Internet obsessively for information on my husband's girlfriend, actual stalking was unappealing. This was mostly due to proximity, or rather the lack of it, since I'd heard they were in New Jersey. And we'd made a deal: I got

Brooklyn, he got New Jersey. I considered this about the best exchange since the U.S. bought Alaska for 1.9 cents an acre from Russia, and I wasn't going to blow it.

And people talked me down a lot.

"Every time you ask him why, it will be fresh wound," Amy told me.

When Amy was going through her divorce, she'd had an affair with her nineteen-year-old intern in the office of the Catholic charity where she worked as a fund-raiser.

"Didn't you have to evaluate his job performance?" I asked.

"Yep," she said. "I started with 'Clearly this is awkward.'"

"That must have been one popular internship," I told her.

One night when I felt particularly bad, I met a twenty-three-year-old guy at the club I used to go to with my husband. We met while waiting in line for the bathrooms. I learned that he had been born in Venezuela and raised in Turkey. His parents were Christian missionaries, and he was the fifth of ten children.

"Religion is for the scared and ignorant," he declared.

I had said things like that when I was twenty-three — repeatedly — to my religious parents.

On my twenty-first birthday, my grandmother rather cryptically said to me, "This is a great age. You still think that you can do anything." I'm sure I did.

Maybe that's why we go after the young ones in our pain; we want the time when we thought of ourselves as 100 percent right and unconquerable.

Later the missionaries' son and I ended up making out. The kissing morphed into full-on necking in the corner. He wanted to come home with me, but eventually I made a break for it. I located the girlfriend I had come with and we ran outside and jumped into a cab.

The next morning I noticed that he had sent me seven text messages overnight, begging to come over.

I smiled at these and called Amy.

"Do you think they know we're doing this because we're angry and hurt?" she asked.

"Do you think they care?" I answered.

"The thing with the young ones is that I'm afraid of the moment of disillusionment," she said. "When they see your thighs in the full light of day and realize how old you really are."

"You can have chunky thighs at any age," I said. "I think it's when they see you writing text messages, poking at your cell phone with your index finger, that the Oedipal nature of the relationship becomes clear to them."

Another friend, a scientist with a very rational approach to the irrational, advised me, "You should probably keep making out with the twenty-three year olds for as long as you can. Your days are limited."

I brought my attention back to class. Graciela walked around us, speaking in her musical way, as if she were orating an epic poem; she snapped her fingers to the beat and gave us suggestions as we danced.

"There are only three steps in tango: forward, backward, and to the side. With every step," she said, "there must be clarity of intention."

We then got into pairs and practiced sacadas. *Sacar*, in Spanish, means to "take out" or "remove." In tango it's a physical "displacement": Your partner takes your axis by stepping between your feet. Usually the leader is the intruder and the follower's leg is interrupted when he brushes her weightless leg. The intention is to take her spot; her displaced leg flares back, grazing the floor behind her. She has to move on and find a new axis. By the time they are facing each other, he has her old space, but her new axis is all hers; if he wants it, he'll have to physically take it.

I kept moving my leg before the leader brushed it. This is known as "anticipating" the lead. It can cause problems, as the dynamic between the follower and the leader is created by his boldness and her surrender. If the follower anticipates too much, she's pretty much dancing by herself. I had to learn to wait and not to move out of my leader's way before he brushed against me. If the follower doesn't wait, there's no tension and no dynamic.

Graciela yelled, "Stop leading yourself. Just let it happen. When you let the weight go, momentum will take your leg."

We switched partners and I tried not to flinch as I let the next man displace me with a sacada. It started to feel good in the melancholy sense of resigning yourself to what is, accepting the present situation, and then moving on.

After class, students milled about in the lobby: A short man with wide shoulders and a barrel chest spoke Spanish into his cell phone; a woman in a taupe business suit nervously tapped her foot; a man wearing a white turban buffed his dance shoes. They were all waiting for their lessons to begin, and there was no telling into which room they'd disappear—ballroom, tango, hustle, or salsa.

Two people practiced swing dancing in one of the studios: A middle-aged black man and a small, young Latina bopped and twirled honky-tonk. Salsa music poured out of another room, and I saw a few lips moving, counting the steps, then pursed in concentration as people tried to step in time to the music and execute their turns. It reminded me of the line by H. G. Wells, "Every time I see an adult on a bicycle, I no longer despair for the future of the human race." That's how I felt watching adults learn to dance. There's such a childlike earnestness to the process.

An instructor started roaming the hallway, recruiting followers for her American tango class. Usually there were more women than men for classes, but this time it went the other way. I had an hour before my practica started.

"I'll help out, but I'm an Argentine tango student," I explained.

"That's fine," she said. "It's a basic class and we're going to work on the promenade. You'll have no problem.

"We have a few Argentine tango followers here," the instructor announced. "The embrace in ballroom tango is different, in the sense that you lean slightly back and look over your partner's shoulders, not at them. It's meant for show."

Then she giggled and said, "Blame Arthur Murray."

Arthur Murray is at the center of the success story of American dance. Born Moses Teichman to European immigrants, as a young man in New York City he wanted to overcome his shyness by learning to dance. He advanced quickly and began working as a dance instructor. In order to make more money, he studied business and marketing. In the 1920s Murray found a way to capitalize on the dance craze sweeping the United States:

He started advertising mail-order dance lessons. For a nickel, he would send off a footstep diagram of the latest dance. There were fourteen lessons in all. He then started opening dance studios and coined the simple but effective motto "Be Popular, Learn to Dance."

The Arthur Murray dance studios were the first franchise in the United States. At the request of a hotel chain, he sent instructors out to teach dance lessons. When the hotel no longer needed them, the dancers didn't return to New York City but stayed put in each town, and Murray helped them start dance studios. He then managed the advertising nationally in exchange for a percentage of the gross profits. By the time he retired in 1964, he had 350 franchised studios that grossed $25 million a year.

Murray realized that he was cashing in on loneliness. In a 1934 profile of the dance entrepreneur in *The New Yorker*, Milton Mackaye wrote, "Murray didn't choose instructors for their beauty, but for background and personality. There is a sound reason for this. The average man who learns to dance is afraid of beauties; what he seeks is sympathy and understanding, and not a biological bonfire."

Arthur Murray married one of his students, Kathryn, and she became his dance partner as well. Their weekly television show began with the catch phrase "Put a little fun in your life, try dancing."

In the American tango class we walked quick, quick, slow and then rotated partners and continued promenading around the room. This class seemed more humorous to me than groups learning the Argentine tango, in part because American, also called international or ballroom tango, has such a persona of grandeur, which just didn't fit this motley group dressed in their work clothes.

The differences between American and Argentine tango reveal fundamental differences in the cultures. The American promenade is a mostly competitive dance, set to predetermined steps. It is about being seen, about projecting yourself as graceful to an audience. The leader's responsibility to his partner is to make her look good to the audience and judges. Dancers do not hold each other in tight embraces; rather, they keep their torsos at a distance. They do not look at each other, but rather out at the audience. The musical tempo is upbeat, and overall, it's a sweet, innocent dance that radiates optimism.

The Argentine tango, on the other hand, is full of pathos. Couples close in tightly, feeling each other's pulse, each other's pain. They press their foreheads together, like lips in an endless kiss. It's a dance that revels in the drama of suffering, one that says that failure binds us together much more closely than does success.

As a culture, Americans despise failure. The gym in my high school had slogans painted on the walls in huge letters: AMERICAN ENDS IN "I CAN" and FAILURE IS NOT AN OPTION. We carry this mentality with us. Failure makes you a "loser." It doesn't matter how many entrepreneurs reveal their early flops, or how many first marriages end in disasters that lead to better second marriages. Reflection, nostalgia, and melancholy, along with the spectrum of emotions encompassing pain, sorrow, and regret, are acceptable only in country music, the blues, and on occasion other types of music. We may even study failure: In *Hamlet*, Ophelia loses her mind and then dies of a broken heart. The narrator in Song of Solomon suffers unabashedly. Her love psalm is familiar to scorned women: "I opened to my beloved; but my beloved had withdrawn himself, and was gone: my soul failed when he spake: I sought him, but I could not find him; I called him, but he gave me no answer." But not today, not us. We're supposed to hide our mistakes and keep our sorrow secret. Nothing feels more like failure than publicly declaring your love and intention to be together forever in front of family and friends and then crying into your divorce lawyer's answering machine late at night.

This promenade of the American tango was giving everyone something: a change, a way to meet people, a persona to try on. We stepped, quick, quick, slow, looking past each other's shoulders with a smile. But I wanted the other tango, the one for the heartbroken.

Later that night at the practica, I plopped down in the folding chair next to Claire and we gossiped about the other dancers. I spotted Irish Guy, who had gone back to avoiding me by shifting the top half of his body in the opposite direction, as if he were executing an advanced yoga move.

I told Claire what he'd said to me, about my being terrible. "And even though he said I'd improved, he still ignores me. I feel like I failed a test."

"When I first started," Claire said, "some old guy quit after one dance and told me that dancing with me was like trying to move cement around the floor."

"What a bastard," I said.

"It was probably true," Claire said. "But I was devastated."

"The problem with Irish Guy is that he's everywhere," I said. "He doesn't miss a practica, and he says that he goes to a milonga every night of the week."

It was if I had this little beacon of rejection that was always there, whispering "You suck!" There was nothing that got my attention more than a person who didn't like me. I'd brush past admirers or pleasant conversationalists to win over the one who ignored me no matter how odious I might find him or her. It didn't matter if it was a woman who was rude to me at a party or a guy whom I wouldn't under other circumstances think twice about. I had to make them all like me. I recognized that this need was a huge waste of time and energy, but I couldn't help myself. Now Irish Guy had brought it all back to me. There was nothing particularly attractive about him except that he didn't want to dance with me.

"And he's Irish American—my people," I said to Claire. "They usually like me."

Claire laughed. "Maybe he has a crush on you."

"Maybe he's gay," I said.

"I'm going to die alone," Claire said. "I had a date last night and just blew it."

Claire had been trying not to emasculate her dates. She frequently opened doors for both of them, decided what they would do, where they would eat, and insisted on paying half the bill.

"Not only did I split the check," she said. "I decided the tip he left wasn't adequate and added more. Right in front of him."

"Well, at least you're aware that you're doing it," I said. "That means you can stop, right?"

"I don't seem to be able to. I think I want a guy who can take charge, and then I don't allow it."

Allen arrived and sat down next to us. We all watched an old man in a veteran's cap bounce around the dance floor.

"I wonder what war he fought in," I commented. "Or maybe it's just a look . . . sort of a 'proud to be conservative' thing."

"I used to be a Young Republican," Allen said. "I converted to Christianity about that time."

"How'd your Jewish parents like that?" I asked.

"My dad just said, 'Sure, you're a Christian.' But it got a rise out of my mother. She cried a few times."

"That's a sweet story," Claire said. "I just did it again, didn't I? I didn't mean to say sweet. Maybe cute. No, not that either. I don't know what I mean. Let's dance, Allen."

As they settled into the embrace, I mouthed at her, "Let him lead."

Claire laughed.

I watched Allen and Claire start into the basic. Earlier Claire had revealed that her father had left her family when she was about a year old. Her mother struggled to raise her and her sister on food stamps. Her distrust of men started long before her ex-boyfriend cheated on her.

Just then Peter, dressed in faded jeans and a muted aqua blue

T-shirt that set off his eyes, walked in. He had an expressive way of entering the room, and he always seemed to be carrying bags—sometimes filled with clothes and dance shoes, along with his laptop and, usually, food. He ate continuously. When he spotted someone he knew, he'd scurry toward them on his tiptoes, laughing. Today, though, he just headed straight for the corner and changed his clothes in a flurry. We caught each other's eyes and smiled.

A couple approached him and I overheard him talking about his film. "Making a film" is a loose term. Peter had completed a short trailer, but as far as I could tell, he spent his days in coffee shops, laptop open, hoping a movie star or rich producer would walk by and offer to fund his project. There was some multitasking involved, as he simultaneously waited for friends of friends and cousins of uncles who knew somebody who wanted to make a film on gay tango and would collaborate with him. This meant they would pony up the money.

When he was done talking, Peter came and sat down next to me.

"Potential film funders?" I asked.

"No, or most likely not," he said. "I don't know why, but each time I have to tell someone that the movie is about gay tango, I cringe a little while I wait for their response."

"You don't want to be judged," I said.

He nodded. "Probably."

After Peter tied his laces, he led me to the center of the floor. We started in open embrace, but he moved me so that I stood right at his side. He placed his foot at the outside of mine, pulled my full weight against him, and then whispered, "Relax." I was plank stiff, leaning against him.

"Even though you're just learning, you're fun to dance with," he said. "You don't care if I add moves that aren't really tango."

"That wasn't a tango step?" I asked.

"No, I made it up."

I came to learn that Peter improvised a lot; he had trained as a modern dancer, and we liked to just walk, side by side, hitting beats as our feet landed. He'd spin me and I'd spot myself the way I had learned in salsa. When I danced with Peter I forgot about worrying; I just let go, realizing that I was really dancing—fully in the moment, like a meditation—and when I lost myself like that, I stopped caring how I looked or who was watching.

The song "Libertango," by Astor Piazzolla, came on and Peter grabbed me again. We walked, hitting the beat. Then he added a syncopation and also stepped on the off-beat; our legs battled and synchronized at the same time. Piazzolla was one of Argentina's greatest composers. Though many of this compositions are not danceable, his influence on contemporary tango is immense and also ties New York to the evolution of this music and dance. Piazzolla's family moved from the Mar de la Plata in Argentina to New York City in 1925, when he was four years old. He spent a good portion of his childhood learning classical music from his next-door neighbor, Hungarian pianist Béla Wilda, who had studied with the great Sergei Rachmaninoff. It was also the time of the Harlem Renaissance, and the jazz played then would later influence Piazzolla. He met Carlos Gardel, the leading singer of tango, when Gardel was at the height of his fame. Gardel took a liking to him and let Piazzolla accompany him on shopping trips around New York. Piazzolla translated for the great singer and occasionally played the bandoneón for Gardel, who let him act the part of a newspaper boy in his film *El Día que Me Quieras* (The Day You Love Me).

Audiences throughout Latin America packed movie houses for the Spanish-language musicals in which Gardel starred, oftentimes insisting that the scenes in which he sang be rewound for encores. Gardel's voice relayed the laments of a million sorrows and immeasurable heartbreak; it was bigger than his brief, remarkable life. He died in 1935 at the peak of his career, when his plane crashed in Colombia. This sent the South American continent into grieving, and Gardel was canonized as the unofficial saint of the Southern Hemisphere and guardian angel of the milonga.

The tango waned after that, but it wasn't due only to Gardel's death. In the 1930s the Great Depression had hit the United States, and more people gathered in food lines than in dance halls. The Depression affected Argentina as well, and this, coupled with the 1930 military coup that forced President Hipólito Yrigoyen from power, created a somber and repressive atmosphere.

Still, Piazzolla carried on, playing in Argentina, Europe, Latin America, and the United States. His music evolved into something sophisticated that was meant to be listened to, not danced to. In many of Piazzolla's later compositions the tango rhythm is vague and difficult to dance to because of the jazz and classical riffs. Traditional tangueros hated him and believed he was polluting their beloved music. Even Argentinean writer Jorge Luis Borges, who might himself be considered avant-garde, allegedly stormed out of a Piazzolla concert in 1960, saying, "I'm leaving. They aren't playing tangos today." (The two geniuses would later collaborate.)

"Libertango," however, is very danceable and perfect for someone like Peter, who makes up his own steps and blurs the boundaries of tradition. After the song ended, Peter and I practiced sacadas. When I anticipated, he reminded me to wait until his leg touched mine.

"I think I might have restless leg syndrome," I joked.

"Aren't there meds for that?" he asked.

"I've seen ads, but the side effects sound terrible."

When I finally gave myself over to waiting, the leg that had been displaced almost swung back behind me on its own. The beauty of the move—the woman's motion comes from a practically involuntary swing—is a little tragic. (Imagine a French film with the main character walking away in the rain and not looking back. The subtitle reads: "This dance step is the sad realization that two people can never truly share the same axis.")

Peter and I saw Dario start to dance a sacada sequence, or a *cadena* (a chain) with a student from his performance class. He would step into her space and do a sacada, then as they spun together she would in turn step into his space and displace him.

They'd make a half turn and a sacada, then they'd spin again, making their way around the room, never stopping for the basic, just taking each other's axis, spinning, then taking it again.

"We have to try that," Peter said.

We followed the line of dance around the room, spinning our small sacadas. I started to understand why Graciela said that the only steps in tango are the side, forward, and back step and all tango dance sequences are a variation of these. Believers in chaos theory locate logic in the seemingly random and disorderly—to find this logic, you have to identify the sequences, or the fractals, which create patterns. Tango is about fractals; the steps are essentially triangles of different shapes and sizes. These fixed patterns, set to melodies and harmonies, give order in the chaos of emotions. Patterns are what we follow to find the source, and in tango, the source is why a person chooses this dance.

A storm will leave wreckage, in which we can see its fractal pattern. In this way the tempest tells its story. The repetition of patterns is what we perceive as harmony in the natural order. It is beauty in its most sublime form. People usually prefer subtle variations on a theme to abrupt change and, as in music, favor harmony over discord. This is why tangueros objected to Piazzolla's discordant sounds. Harmony makes us believe that all is well in our universe, and even though we might be picking through the flotsam of a storm, we still find comfort in pattern.

Fractal patterns in nature can be refined further and further: the storm to the coastline, the coastline to the boulder, the boulder to the fossil of a shell embedded in it, the fossil to the microscopic pieces of minerals, the mica and oxide in volcanic stone. Smaller and smaller pieces of the story are fractal patterns, leading back to that initial, singular spark in the primordial puddle.

We can follow these patterns in our lives and trace them back. Claire's betrayal by her boyfriend is merely the larger part of the wreckage left by her father. Peter's shame at telling people he's making a film about gay men, his fear of being judged, goes back to many other moments in his life. Allen's desire to learn how to talk with women, to take them in his arms, comes after what were probably many mishaps and embarrassments. For me, marrying a man who wasn't committed to me, who didn't love me fully, goes back to my seeking approval from those who are least likely to give it. I wanted to change this. The dance steps give us the route back to the sources of human sorrow and human happiness. And if sorrow can duplicate itself, then happiness must be able to do so as well. If we follow a different pattern or find a new rhythm, then a new sequence, a new cadena, can be formed.

CHAPTER 7

El Gancho, The Hook

SOME MEN LIKE the woman's gancho to be hard and smile at the erotic impulse of a woman's leg snapping against theirs. Others prefer a more sedate gancho, a gentle swing of the follower's leg hooking into theirs. Usually it isn't a slow, seductive move; rather, it's saucy and a little dangerous. Imagine a hit, a kiss, a hug, a slap.

You learn the gancho by teetering on one foot (which is stuck in a two-inch stiletto) like a precarious stork. When you feel your partner bend his leg and twist his torso, you wind your upper body around his and try to relax your legs and let them swing, based on the motion of your leader and the energy he exerts. Adapting to one man is hard enough, never mind adjusting to many men. Irish Guy had wanted me to do it so he could really feel it.

"But my high heel could really hurt you," I said. "Safety first. Then when I learn it, I will gancho you like a cowgirl." Hipster liked one slow, soft flick of the heel that involved a sexy winding of legs, and Martial Artist informed me that he really didn't like the gancho much at all. "Just because I know it doesn't mean I have to use it," he said. "I'm mastering the unvalued art of restraint," he said.

"Think of colors as you hear the music," Graciela said. "If it's a sharp, clear beat, think red. Staccato. Heat. If it's long and melodic, lead it white. Soothing and clear." We rotated partners and I tried the gancho with short men and then tall; they led it gently or firmly, brittlely or flexibly; some led it red, some white, and lots blundered through it in a confounding shade of pink. The gancho requires understanding a man's intention, inferring his desires, and learning how he likes it to feel — it's too soft for one, too hard for the next. No wonder this dance came from the brothels.

I used tango to prepare myself for dating again, to understand the intricacies of romantic negotiation. Friends had convinced me that the fastest way to recover from divorce would be to Internet date. Since I had stopped crying in public, I figured that I was ready. I went over to Amy and Isaac's to write an online profile. I wanted both a male and a female perspective — it was marketing, after all. I looked over the Craigslist personals for Men Looking for Women and was aghast.

WARM OIL MASSAGE FOR A WOMAN WITH
CURVES — 38 (MANHATTAN)
YOUR SEXY SECRET LOVER — 32 (NYC)
LARGE NIPPLE FETISH
YOU + ME = PHOTO

Finally I burst out laughing. "No way. I can't do this," I told Amy.

"Oh, that site is for sex workers," Amy said. "Normal people don't go to Craigslist." We poured ourselves more wine and looked over some tamer dating sites. It was like catalogue shopping. We came across a man dressed in hunting camouflage fatigues who appeared to be holding a large gun. He was looking for someone who was "kind and compassionate."

"To go kill animals with," I said.

We laughed at the many poorly cropped images. Men had simply cut out ex-girlfriends, but something always remained, a hand or a strand of hair. Then we found a skinny bald guy standing on a boulder with his knobby knees exposed, who had listed "simultaneous orgasms" as something he couldn't live without, and we had to wipe tears from our eyes.

Amy told me about Isaac's personal ad. They actually met through mutual friends, but at the time, Isaac had an online dating profile. He was a catch, handsome and intelligent, but didn't get one response. Apparently a friend "styled" him and helped him write his entry. For his picture he wore a shiny disco shirt and his hair was shaped into a pompadour. Amy told me that the profile ended with the catch phrase "Doesn't anyone out there want to get their funk on?" We laughed so hard we pounded the table.

The unspoken rules are that guys who don't mention sex in their profile are likely to get more dates, and women should never mention marriage or babies. But over and over again, these rules were broken. As we perused both sexes' profiles I learned something I had never known about New Yorkers: They all loved the outdoors—none were indoorsy. Odd for the most crowded, urban metropolis in the United States, where people prized their expensive shoes. There were also a surprising number of jazz lovers.

Isaac warned me against mentioning dancing: He believed it would scare men off. They might think that I expected a boyfriend to learn to do it. I just slipped a reference in once, when filling in the blanks on one site. "_____ is sexy . . . but _____ is sexier." I typed in "salsa" then "tango."

I posted my personal ad and waited. It felt kind of like dropping a fishing pole in the water, then wandering off to do something else while it bobbed.

At the practica, I kept focused on getting ready to date. I stood at the side of the floor, waiting to be asked to dance. I wanted to look open but not too eager. I caught myself folding my arms across my chest. This defensive stance was surely a deterrent; I dropped my arms and tried to look alert. When men passed by without making eye contact, I folded my arms back across my chest. Then, after standing alone for a few moments, I let them dangle.

I had learned about certain body language, mostly from teaching. I had walked into my freshman composition classroom, a required course, and observed my students slouching in their seats, heads nodding toward their chests from drowsiness, jaws slack, and announced, "If I knew how to read body language, I'm sure I'd be offended right now." In creative writing classes, an elective, everyone was sitting at attention, shoulders squared, ready to go.

I was unsure of what posture meant "available but not desperate" at the side of a dance floor. Dance is a coded language. The steps are the vocabulary and grammar; the sequences that come from putting steps together are the syntax. Once, years ago when I was learning the mambo jazz step at a salsa class, I was reminded of Emily Dickinson's poems. I was teaching an introduction to literature survey course at the time. The salsa jazz step ends abruptly, on an off-beat, and it felt like the syntax Dickinson might use: "A poor—torn heart—a tattered heart—"

In various styles of tango songs, I could hear some of the poets whom I had taught to many a listless student: In the songs that hit a strong, fast beat, there's the meter of John Donne's "Death be not proud, though some have called thee." More melodious songs reminded me of the sexy alliteration of Walt Whitman, such as "Only the lull I like, the hum of your valved voice." And the gancho? The sharp, snappy hook? It can be upbeat or angry or sexy, like the Dylan Thomas poem "Do Not Go Gentle into that Good Night."

In language, what places you in time and space are verbs (passive or active), participles, and gerunds. In dance it's rhythm that moves you: tempo, accent, meter, and flow. It has often been said that dance is more similar to poetry than to prose. (Hence the upsurge in poetry sales in 1913 London.)

Dances, the two-step, hustle, salsa, swing, all have their own rules, which are understood by those who know the "language." To communicate, you learn the steps, build them into patterns, and commit them to memory. You must be part of the group to participate. The natural world requires this as well.

Each honeybee hive has its own dance, its own language, so bees can communicate to one another where the flowers with the most nectar are to be found. They dance the direction and the distance to the flowers on the honeycomb, making a map. German bees dance a different language from Italian and Egyptian bees. Each hive has its own dialect and creates its own scent. If a bee does not carry this scent or does not know the language of a hive it tries to enter, the guard bees kill it.

Dance classes are ways to learn a common language. But even with a shared vocabulary, some gaps in communication remain. How do you attract men you want to dance with but not those whom you don't? What do you do with your hands? Hands on hips means aggression. Hand to cheek signifies evaluation. Pulling or tugging at ears indicates indecision. Rubbing the eyes is doubt. What gesture means "I'd like to be asked to dance by a preintermediate guy who smells okay?"

I sucked in my stomach and softened my face muscles — not a smile, not a frown. A man looked toward me, and I maintained eye contact. He approached.

"I'm Dave," he said. "I'm a little tall for you, so just rest your hand on my shoulder."

Keeping open embrace was considerate. When a tall man pulled me into a close embrace, I had to stretch out, strain my legs upward to match the man's height, then extend them as far as I could so we wouldn't bump legs and I could meet his stride. Dave knew I was a beginner and tailored his dancing to me. But I still let my mind wander, missed a step, and apologized.

"Listen," he said. "Don't say you're sorry. There are only two things a man wants when he dances with you. He wants you to want to dance with him more than any other man. He wants to impress you. You don't have to do anything. I once had a tango instructor who would just stop dancing if she didn't understand something. She didn't apologize for not knowing how to follow; rather, she'd demand to be led clearly."

I met my first Internet date, M., at an Italian wine bar in my neighborhood. Amy used to take her dates there, and if she liked them, they would go to a darker bar a few blocks away to make out. (Isaac was still angry that he was taken on this "pony trot.") I waited for M. at a corner table where candlelight flickered off the exposed-brick walls. Wood beams ran along the ceiling. He arrived and apologized for being late. Along with physical gestures, there are also social codes in dating: His traveling to my neighborhood was a good sign, but for a woman to sit alone in a bar or restaurant waiting for her date to arrive is a bad beginning. The problem is, not everyone shares these codes. He might have thought this made him look fashionable. I thought it made him seem rude.

Once M. was seated, we ordered two glasses of wine and decided to share a cheese plate. The conversation moved comfortably enough. He looked like the picture in his profile and appeared not to have lied about his age, but something kept him from being handsome. I thought it was around his jaw, an overbite maybe. Soon I realized it was his lack of confidence. He seemed uncomfortable in his own skin, and his posture at the table was slightly defensive. On paper he was fine: belonged to a natural-food co-op, was passionate about cooking, and had a job he didn't like that paid well. He expressed envy that I worked as a writer.

"Well, aren't you lucky," he said. "I guess that requires a trust fund."

I was a little taken aback at the snarkiness.

"No," I answered. "I've been doing it for some time now. And I teach off and on."

"Oh, really, like grade school?" he asked.

"College" I said. "But lately I've had enough assignments to stop teaching for a little while."

There was no spark. In fact, I found the wedges of mild sheep cheese dotted with black truffles and the chunks of sharp Romano far more exciting than my date. I started thinking about how I would extract myself from this politely. In tango, you dance three to five songs to learn about each other. The first can be a little awkward, the second better, the third lets the connection meld. Of course, sometimes you wanted to run away from him after the first song: He's off the beat, has bad breath, pushes you with his hand instead of inviting you with his chest. Women bolder than I do this; they politely beg off after one song, saying they need a drink of water. Men had done it to me, but I couldn't do it. I still blamed myself for any bad dancing and worried too much about hurting other people's feelings.

While pondering polite ways to tell this man there wouldn't be a second date, I realized that he wasn't even a bit interested in me. This didn't seem acceptable. Why wouldn't he be? What was wrong with me? The urge to win him over welled up, and while I told myself that I wasn't interested in this angry, insecure man, another part of me—the desperate part that needs to be liked by everyone—clicked in, and I caught myself tilting my head, an invitation in the body-language world to "come closer." I made eye contact and smiled.

Stop it, I told myself. You don't even want to see him again.

With a force of will, I straightened my head and started tapping a foot and cut off any type of physical coquettishness.

When the bill came, he flipped it over and said, "So, should we split this?"

A CAGEY CROWD surrounded the dancers gathered in the Chelsea Market. A thin rope had been strung to create a makeshift dance floor and keep the tango dancers separate from the shoppers and the young women giving away gelato samples. This Saturday-afternoon milonga had attracted close to a hundred dancers. As evening approached and the shops closed, the lines were taken down and the dancers spread out through the mall, dancing in front of the seafood shop and bakery. I waited on the sidelines until a man shaped like a pumpkin invited me to dance. My chin hovered just above his thin white hair, and I took in his sweet, musky smell. That old, round guy moved like butter, and we glided around the floor. Seamless and silky, he pulled me inside the music and it felt so good.

He led me through a basic crossover and then a subtle, gentle gancho, and we ended standing parallel. Before the second song he said, "Move more slowly, wait for me. I want to make you look beautiful. That's my job."

In partner dancing and dating, chemistry is the central component. This small, rotund man was not someone I would want to go on a date with. I knew little of his personality except what I learned from dancing with him. He had nice manners, but that's not physical attractiveness. I felt chemistry with him anyway, though, a warm connection like a soft hum between us that created an almost narcotic flush. We can all have chemistry with people who are not appropriate mates and then have no chemistry with those who might be good matches. A few of the dating websites have hired experts to break it down and try to define it so people can make better matches.

The anthropologist Helen Fischer was hired by an Internet dating service to help match prospective singles. She believes that women are unconsciously attracted to men with a different immune system, which they sort out through the sense of scent. According to Fischer, this would produce offspring who are genetically more varied, which is good for our evolution. She believes that the four basic chemical systems, dopamine, serotonin, estrogen, and testosterone, are associated with Plato's temperaments: the Artist, the Guardian, the Idealist, and the Rationalist.

While estrogen and testosterone are hormones, some scientists believe they may act as pheromones. These are signals that enter the brain, possibly through scent, that can trigger the libido, as well as stimulating fear and aggression. (Honeybees release pheromones to communicate to their swarm.) Another chemical transaction associated with love and sex involves the neurotransmitter dopamine. But why does one particular person, and not the next, set off a certain chemical reaction?

Fischer gave 1.6 million men and women a questionnaire. She created her own categories based on Plato's: The explorers were risk takers, which is associated with dopamine. The builders tend to be social and follow rules; they had dominant serotonin pathways. Verbally skilled negotiators were heavy on estrogen. Directors, outwardly competitive and direct, were in the testosterone category (surprise, surprise). She found that people with lots of serotonin were attracted to people who are heavy on dopamine. I imagine the same could apply for estrogen and testosterone. In Internet dating, when men claim they want "a woman who looks good in jeans as well as an evening dress" and women say they want "honesty and no games," what they really want is someone who doesn't smell like them.

My line on the Internet dating site was getting some bites, and I agreed to go on a date with W., a Brazilian who worked at the United Nations. He seemed polite and worldly. He invited me to the nicest *churrascaria*, or Brazilian steakhouse, in town. I trusted that he would pay; I had never been out with a Latin man who hadn't. He was there waiting for me. He held my chair and insisted I order first. I love good manners.

The waiters came by with skewers of filet mignon, chorizo, and prime rib. And then the side dishes started arriving: grated yucca flowers, onion rings flecked with herbs, and deep-fried bananas that I relished in small, sweet bursts between nibbles of salty meat. The waiter poured us glasses of Cabernet Sauvignon. It was all perfect until the luxury was interrupted by the very sad story of this man's life.

His parents divorced when he was five, and his father fought to get full custody of his children. He accused his wife of having an affair. The judge ruled that she was an adulteress. Years later, on the one occasion when he saw his mother, she would explain that the judge blackmailed her by saying that he would award her custody of her children if she slept with him. So she did, thereby proving to the judge that she was in fact unfaithful. The judge awarded the children to her husband. Ill equipped to handle children on his own, W.'s father parceled W. and his sister out to relatives. By the age of fifteen, he was living on his own.

I felt so sorry for his mother and those children that I lost my appetite.

After dinner we caught a taxicab and headed downtown to a club where a Cuban group was playing. W. confessed that this was his first date since his divorce. While it wasn't my first, it

was the first time I'd gone out to dance salsa since my separation. This might not have been such a great idea. Watching
W. jumping around, his stiff, small torso boxlike in his business suit, made me miss dancing with my husband, the smooth
hips, the sexy shoulder shakes, the firm hand on my back. W.
bounced toward me and tried to cop a quick, unwelcomed kiss,
but I backed up and he missed. I knew there wouldn't be a second date with him. Sympathy isn't attraction. And I didn't feel
guilty. He had his first date since his divorce and it wasn't bad,
and sometimes what we need is to relearn this stuff one small
step at a time.

So it was back to the dance floor to try and become wiser
about dating. Dancing is something you can learn, but attraction is a big unknown. At one practica I danced with a man
who had started learning tango at the same time I had. He was
originally from Turkey, where tango has been wildly popular
since the early 1900s. He had wonderful posture, keeping his
chest forward, wide and generous, so that I could stay connected
to him. He smelled slightly of aftershave, earthy and floral at the
same time. He held me close but gave me room to move when
he led a back ocho. We mostly just tango walked, but a good
caminita can feel wonderful. As we moved through the second
and third song, I realized that something between us didn't connect. The problem was not our timing and not our strides, but
that he was nervous. He exhaled in short clips and our pulses,
our breathing never aligned. Graciela had warned about this: If
you aren't relaxed, the connection can't happen.

By the second song of the tanda he exhaled, and at the third, we breathed in sync as we walked, bringing about that magical melding. When the set ended, we parted. I sat on the side and fanned myself for a moment, thinking that I danced best with men closest to my height. At first I thought it was simply compatible leg length, but then I began to understand that when our chests were evenly aligned, I could feel my own heart. Chemistry with another person can also mean becoming acquainted with what is best about yourself. Though this critical organ should be familiar to us, the gentle, inexplicable sensation of actually experiencing it is anything but. To feel the other person's heartbeat mingle with your own — that's a pleasure that's hard to leave. St. Augustine wrote, "The hairs of his head are easier by far to count than his feeling, the movements of his heart." Scientists can locate the chemicals, but what the heart craves remains a mystery.

Dating can be like a tanda that allows a second, third, even fourth song so that a couple can find the connection when dancing. So I made a second date with L. Our first date had been at a small wine bar in the East Village. He worked with computers but had a graduate degree in English, so he had a steady paycheck and was well read. We talked about books we liked and former colleagues of mine with whom he had studied. L. had kind hazel eyes flecked with green, prematurely gray hair, and ears that stuck out. We laughed a lot through the evening. He had bought the wine, to me a signal that he liked me. Later, through e-mails, we agreed to meet a second time.

The second date, like dancing the second song in a tanda,

is very telling. Any doubts you had during the first one would be either confirmed or dispelled. And I did have a few doubts about L. He had spent a rather long time telling me about his ex-girlfriend, who "had a great heart but some emotional problems." She screamed and yelled and threw things. She took lots of antidepressants but still had an eating disorder and had never recovered from the abuse of her alcoholic father. She swung between rage and depression. He said that he finally couldn't take it. I wondered why he was telling me all this on a first date.

"He sounds emotionally promiscuous," a friend told me. "Watch out for that."

L. arrived late to our second date, at a Spanish tapas bar. That's when he told me that he had started writing poetry and composing folk songs to perform at open mike night. "Sometimes I read my poetry, but sometimes I go up there with my guitar," he said. "Either way, I just like to step up to the microphone and put myself out there. I'd really like it if you came and watched me sometime."

Definitely promiscuous. I had a strong inkling that open mike night would be the end for us. I thought it would be better to stop now and not have to squirm through that experience.

I went to the bathroom and called Claire.

"Hey, I'm still at work," she said. "I have a big meeting with clients coming up."

"When you finish, you want to go dance tonight?" I asked her.

"It's like you're inside my brain," she said.

"I hang out there a lot," I told her. "Just so you know."

She laughed and said, "Stay in the light and away from the dark, shadowy places. Want to meet in the East Village?"

I returned to the sangria and my date. He was a nice guy. I wanted him to know I thought that, but he wasn't right for me. Back then, probably nobody was. I thanked him for the date, insisted on paying our bill, and hurried to a milonga taking place nearby in the back room of a Ukrainian restaurant.

The crowd was the usual mix of couples, along with Irish Guy, a few leaders from Turkey, some women from my studio, and a small gang of Argentinean women. These tango mavens had zero body fat, jet-black hair, and fabulous outfits. They danced with equally skilled men whose feet slid preternaturally over the floor as if caressing it.

I felt a light tap on my shoulder and was relieved to find it was Claire.

"I never thought that I'd say this, but I just want to close my eyes and let a man lead me around," she said. "I'm exhausted. I've been negotiating with the contractors all day on this project. It's not really my job, but the clients keep calling me."

"I had a date," I told her. "It didn't go so well."

"Why not?" she asked.

"I don't know," I told her. "He's into reading poetry and playing his guitar at open mikes and he wanted me to go."

"Ooh. That's bold on his part," she said. "Look, you're probably not ready. You're not even officially divorced yet. It all takes a while."

I spotted a few guys from class and danced with one of them. There wasn't "chemistry," but dancing with them was pleasant, safe. That's all I wanted. Afterward I went and stood on the sidelines.

Claire came over and nudged me.

"You okay?" she asked.

"Yeah," I said. "How's your evening going?"

"I hate being a beginner," she said. "Sometimes I feel like I'm improving, then I lose it all and start fumbling."

"Take it easy on yourself," I said.

"I don't think I can do that," she said.

"It's just dancing," I said.

"You don't really believe that," she answered.

"No, but I keep telling myself I do," I said.

We both left a little after midnight and walked to the subway, clutching our bags, which bulged with dance shoes.

Later that night I checked my e-mails. A married man—he'd stated it clearly on his profile—had contacted me through the dating site. His "photo" was just a black-and-white drawing of an eye. I wanted to send him a nasty message, tell him how he's going to ruin his wife's life, but I didn't. Very late that night my phone rang, and when I answered, the caller didn't say a word; it was the void, that place to which my husband, the life I had imagined for myself, had disappeared.

The next day I took down my profile and started dressing for a milonga. Black underwear, black bra, black hose, black skirt, black top, black shoes. Once at the milonga, I changed shoes and then stood on the edge of the dance floor, arms crossed to warm myself. Then I remembered to let them dangle and waited to be asked to dance. Here, it was no longer New York City but any city; the tango music pushed back the world outside as the lyrics of "Donde Estás Corazón," sung in a high throaty call by Teresita Asprella, dominated the room. "*¿Donde estás corazón? / No oigo tu palpitar, / Es tan grande el dolor / que no puedo llorar. / Yo quisiera llorar y no tengo más llanto / la quería yo tanto y se fue para no retornar.*" (Where are you, my heart? / I don't hear your beat / My pain is so great / that I can't even cry. / I wish I could cry / but I have no more tears / All this love that I had for him and he left me never to return.)

CHAPTER 8

La Volcada, The Fall

CLAIRE AND I met at the subway station between our apartments and headed into Manhattan for a Friday-night milonga.

"Whenever I buy clothes now," Claire said, "I think, Can I use these for tango? and if the answer is no, I don't buy them."

"I think I have to start wearing totally flat shoes in my everyday life," I said. "To save my feet for tango."

"That's a good idea," she answered. "I need new dancing shoes. The suede wore right off my last pair."

The people with whom Claire shared an office referred to it as the Tango Hole; when she started talking about tango, she couldn't stop. This phrase is also used when friends disappear, as in "Have you seen Fred lately? No, he's gone into the Tango Hole." The tanguero, no longer interested in dinner parties, cocktail hours, and theater tickets, goes dancing every night.

Some friends understood. When I started salsa, I took a balanced approach. I saw my friends on certain nights, danced a few times a week. And I advanced much more slowly because of it. This time I'd be available for weekend brunch with nondancers, but not much else.

At Eighth Avenue, Claire and I got off the subway and started walking toward a brick building shaped like an isosceles triangle and wedged into a corner of a busy intersection. Traffic flowed on all sides of it. The meatpacking district didn't smell of animal offal as it once did, and the catcalls of suspiciously large-boned ladies-of-the-night no longer filled the air. Rather, Hummer limousines dropped off bar hoppers, and beautiful people stomped down the streets in weather-defying fashions. Glancing through windows of dimly lit restaurants, we saw well-heeled customers pick at small platefuls of food. This did not concern us.

We rang the bell, and when someone answered the intercom we both yelled, "Tango!" We climbed the three flights of stairs to the dance studio, Triangulo, which had been named for the building and the dance as well—the steps, at least in essence, outline acute triangles. Glints from strings of white lights hung along an exposed-brick wall reflected in the mirrors on the opposite wall. The windows overlooked the busy streets and sidewalks, and sometimes the air of intrigue, the thrill of the night, floated up to us from the partyers below. On Fridays we were a small, insular crowd, tucked away in our private little boomerang-shaped corner.

Peter came hurrying toward me. "Where have you been?" he asked. "Nobody wants to dance with me."

"Who did you ask?" I answered, surveying the room.

"That guy over there," he said. He pointed to a large, burly Russian man.

"I wouldn't take that too personally," I told him. "Ask a woman."

As I changed shoes, I noticed the couple we most enjoyed watching. Their dancing bordered on the violent; every step, every kick, every spark of contact smoldered with lust.

"Their ganchos are so high, some places ask them to leave," Peter had told me.

The woman wore a plaid super-miniskirt and wielded her salmon pink, spiked dance heels like a martial artist. Her partner twirled her once, and when her back was to his stomach, she whipped her leg up between his and we could hear it make contact with his back. We all winced a little at the thump of impact. They both began to kick ganchos; their legs hooked, then they spun together. In a very untraditional move, they went from face-to-face to grasping the pole in the center of the room and swinging around it.

"The gossip is that she's married but they are having a torrid affair," Peter whispered to me.

"Wonder what she is telling her husband when she's leaving the house dressed in that getup?" I mused.

By this time she had tied up her tank top to reveal her lean torso. She was a flurry of legs, stomach, and breasts, spinning around her partner, as if she were the flames of a fire and he were tied to a stake in the center of it. Oh, but he looked like he was enjoying himself. At first we laughed but then stopped and stared in respect. They turned in a smooth arc, her body as stiff as a plank when she faced away from him.

Allen joined us. "I asked her to dance once."

We didn't mean to hurt his feelings, but both Peter and I started chuckling. We couldn't imagine Allen with such a partner, and in fact, he had learned that she danced with only one man. They had become this singular phenomenon. Over the course of the evening they spoke to no one else, acknowledged no one else. Still, we respected Allen for trying out his newfound boldness by approaching Tango Dominatrix.

"Ambitious," I said. "And kind of punishment-seeking."

"I hadn't seen her dance yet," he admitted.

Just then she spun, whipped her leg up through her partner's spread legs, and almost whacked him on the back with her foot.

"Enough watching. We've got to learn the *volcada*," Peter said, and took me out to the floor.

I once considered this "falling step" to be my Holy Grail, a movement so achingly beautiful I thought I would be content to just know it. The man steps backward, pulling the woman off her axis, and her full weight presses against him; her free leg extends and searches, making a sweep of the area where he once stood. There is something so vulnerable and touching in that moment; the yearning it expresses was almost unbearable to watch.

Neither Peter nor I had been formally taught the volcada in class, so when he stepped back and pulled me off my axis, my lower back jackknifed and I gasped in pain. It didn't feel poetic, just wrong. But I sucked in my breath and we tried a few more times, until he finally said, "Stop grimacing."

"We can't be doing this right," I said, "or followers would all be in back braces."

We noticed a couple who took the tango very seriously. They were always practicing and working on one step or another. Peter knew them and asked the guy to demonstrate. The man led me through the step, and when my back buckled, he said, "You have to engage your abs for this. Really engage."

Afterward Peter spoke with the man, who said: "We're going to the tango festival in Buenos Aires. We registered for four classes a day. It's not going to be a relaxing vacation; we know it's going to be a lot of work but worth it."

When he danced off, I commented to Peter, "Oh, brother, they aren't even professional dancers. 'A working vacation . . . '? That's crazy."

"It's about being the best at what you do," Peter said.

"Such a New York City attitude to life," I said. "Even at hobbies everyone is so ambitious."

Peter replied, "Come on. We need to get ready for the Gay Olympics. I'm sure tango is considered a sport there."

I laughed and we made our way to the floor and into the line of dance. During the volcada Peter slid backward, as his shoes had no grip, and since I was off my axis, I couldn't help right us. We started sliding to the floor, our chests connected, our legs slipping out behind us. At the last moment, Peter caught a pole with one hand and slowly walked us back to upright.

"Whew," I said. "That was close."

Then I spotted a man with whom I loved dancing and noticed that his girlfriend wasn't around. He was like my tango secret lover: We were having an approximation of an affair at the milongas. When she hadn't shown up yet, or had gone to the bathroom or danced with someone else, we sought each other out. He danced close embrace, with steady steps broken occasionally by long strides; then he walked in a quick, syncopated pattern. Slightly shorter than I am, he had a round chest that was easy to lean into. His blond hair stuck out in stiff strands, and by this time in the evening he usually had to mop the sweat from his brow with a handkerchief. His girlfriend certainly had nothing to worry about off the dance floor, but each time I leaned into his chest and he wrapped his arms around me and started to walk, I felt like I was falling in clandestine love anew.

"Here, try the volcada with me," he offered. "I have a strong upper body." Since we were in close embrace, he stepped back just a little and I engaged my abs and let my foot make a tiny sweep, then brought it back and crossed it in front of the other one. He walked me through the room and I closed my eyes, oblivious to other dancers, shutting out his girlfriend, who now stood against the wall, arms crossed, staring at the dance floor with a grim expression on her face. I breathed into his embrace and felt all the tingling, the warmth, the danger and pleasure of love. When the tanda ended, he bowed slightly and kissed my hand.

Another man asked me to dance. I tried to relax into his

embrace, but he had me too close and when he made turns or pivots, his crotch rubbed against me. During the second song, he turned his head and licked my ear. I froze, pushed myself back from him with both hands, and ran to find Peter, who was having his own problems. His archenemy and rival, Jorge, the man who had started dating his ex-boyfriend in Argentina, was here. Peter grabbed me and pulled me to the dance floor.

"He's not a bad dancer," Peter said. "But he's not cute at all."

We watched Jorge travel over the floor in a smooth glide. He was slight in stature and his dark hair was slicked back. He had an air about him that made him look untrustworthy — though I was biased — and, although not classically handsome, he wasn't ugly. I didn't tell that to Peter.

"You're right," I said. "Not cute at all."

I was privy to the Buenos Aires drama, as I had read Peter's screenplay. I was confused at a few points while reading it, so I'd asked him, "If the characters in the gay tango community in Buenos Aires are really after intimacy and love, why do they keep having sex with pretty much anybody?

Peter said, "Have you ever wanted something so badly that you sabotage it?"

Of course, this broken heart of mine put me in that place; I craved a connection with another person like the one I'd lost, but at the same time I recoiled from it for fear of betrayal. It was worrying about dying of thirst and drowning simultaneously.

"How's fund-raising going?" I asked.

"Oh, one rich man says he'll throw a party to raise money,"

Peter said. "A friend knows a producer who wants to see the trailer and read the script. Same old story, but I have to follow every lead."

"And in the meantime?" I asked.

"Credit cards," he said. "And I've got my job back as a skating Santa for the holiday season."

Peter danced with perturbed, almost staccato movements. He led me into abrupt ganchos, taking out his irritation with quick flicks of his heels.

"This has been a romantic evening all around," I said to him.

"Why? What happened to you?" he asked.

"A gentleman licked my ear while we were dancing," I said.

"What?" Peter stopped dancing. He made me point him out. "What did you do?"

"I was kind of stunned," I said. "I just stopped dancing and walked away."

Just then Martial Artist danced by with a striking woman who moved with otherworldly grace.

"I think I'm going to ask him to dance and lick his ear," Peter said, nodding toward Martial Artist.

"Not if I beat you to it," I answered.

Then the song "Les Jours Tristes," from the soundtrack of the French film *Amélie*, came on, a favorite of Peter's and mine.

We waltzed across the room, laughing like kids on a playground. Modern, or *Nuevo*, tango broke some of the strict rules of traditional tango and blurred the edges with other types of dance, and thus created more opportunity for improvisation. Some dancers prefer classic standards from the belle époque with straightforward steps, and others like to dance nuevo and add new steps, such as volcadas and sacada chains.

It was actually Astor Piazzolla's experimentation with jazz and classical music that triggered the contemporary nuevo tango movement. Nuevo groups fused Argentine tango with popular electronica, giving some classic songs faster, sexier rhythms that could be played either in nightclubs or in tango salons. DJs started mixing in songs by Middle Eastern performers, Delta blues, opera, and Gypsy ballads from Eastern Europe. During its heyday the tango had international influence. Now songs from around the world influenced the tango.

Peter was all nuevo tango; he stepped, scampered, ran, then turned me in a salsa-style spin, and we ended with a gancho. Next he led me into a volcada; then we dropped hands and we danced connected through only our sides. A Tom Waits tango song came and went, next a Nina Simone blues song, followed by the overture from the opera *Don Giovanni*.

Recently my friend Amy had gone to an early Verdi opera. She said that it seemed odd that while the characters were betraying each other, dying of heartbreak and wallowing in misery, the music was lively and upbeat. When she asked her boyfriend, Isaac, a cellist, about it, he explained that it wasn't until Mozart that musical composition emotionally matched the drama taking place. In a way, Mozart was to classical music what Carlos Gardel was to tango. They made the sad tales sound sad.

Astor Piazzolla opened up the tango to jazz and classical influences. He played from the thirties through the fifties, when tango was waning in popularity in many places. In Argentina, though, the dance was revived around the time Juan Perón was first elected president, in 1946. He and his wife, Eva, championed the working class and nationalism, and they promoted tango and Argentine folk music, even restricting imported music. A military coup ousted Perón in 1955, and the new junta viewed with suspicion anything that Perón had encouraged. It imposed curfews and issued edicts banning three or more people from gathering in public, making milongas almost impossible to hold.

Piazzolla, who traveled between Argentina, Europe, and the United States philandering and trying to make a living, seemed unscathed by the political turmoil. Whereas many Argentinean musicians were Peronistas, he disliked the president and resented the expectation that he perform "patriotic" material. "Presidents come and go," he said. "I shall go on playing my bandoneón."

Juan Perón again served as leader of Argentina in 1973, with his new wife, Isabel, as vice president. When he died of a heart attack the following year, Isabel took over as president, but within two years, after a military coup d'état led by General Jorge Videla, the military junta took control of the country. The junta persecuted political dissidents, and thousands of people were kidnapped and executed without trial or record. The tango, which had continued to exist in small pockets throughout Argentina, now waned there as well as abroad.

Worldwide, tango was on the verge of becoming a dusty old relic, when the stage show *Tango Argentina* premiered in Paris in 1983, the year Argentina's military dictatorship fell. Once again the Parisians fell in love with the tango, and a revival was quickly under way as the show toured Europe to sold-out audiences. Another show, *Forever Tango*, opened in San Francisco in 1996, then hit Broadway to great enthusiasm.

When the tanda with Peter ended, my feet hurt, so I went to change out of my heels to flat jazz slippers. Just then a man who spoke with a hint of an Argentine accent appeared and addressed me. "Please put your heels back on. I am a tall man and I want to dance with you."

He was tall indeed, standing at least a foot taller than I. He had a slightly idiosyncratic way of dancing, which, no doubt, he believed to be the best, most authentic way to tango. I concentrated on interpreting his leads until he asked me what I did for a living.

"I'm a writer."

"Oh, very good," he said. "I have a special respect for writers. Do you like it?"

"Most aspects," I said. "It's tough financially."

"Well, in Argentina, women find, how do you say it here, 'sugar daddies' to help them out," he said. "Have you considered that?"

"Not really," I said. "Wouldn't that make me a little too dependent?"

"It would have to be someone you like," he said.

I didn't know if I was being propositioned or if he was just making conversation. He wasn't a bad-looking man. He had a kind face and a full head of dark hair and an average physique. I guessed him to be in his early sixties. I found the idea of being a kept woman humorous, and I had to admit that I was just a little flattered that in my late thirties somebody thought I would make a good mistress.

Later, my potential sugar daddy asked me to dance again and whispered into my ear, "How much would it take? What if he had half a million dollars? Or three quarters of a million. And owned townhouses in Harlem. Would that be enough?"

I laughed and brushed him off but then paused at the mention of that much money. The thought of an ATM receipt that showed a balance with more than three numbers in a row was pretty enticing.

A traditional waltz, or *vals*, came on, so we switched partners and I danced with the Russian man who had rejected Peter earlier. On the first song I was stiff and nervous. By the second, I took deep breaths and let myself relax until he led a sacada. I missed it, then panicked, tried to make it up—which you can't do—and I then started missing his leads.

From the corner of my eye, I saw Irish Guy, almost reclined on a bench, with one leg up, his head resting on his hand. He saw my mistakes. He was right—I sucked.

"Don't think," the Russian man scolded me. "Clear your mind and don't think."

Between songs, I asked him how long he had been dancing.

"Maybe five or six years," he said.

"Did you start here or in Russia?"

"I started lessons here," he answered. "But a lot of Russians dance tango. We are not afraid of sadness."

Some time ago I read an article about Gypsies in Russia who traveled on the trains and, for a fee, predicted the futures of the characters in Mexican soap operas, which were wildly popular in Russia. These *telenovelas* are a shameless form of entertainment: switched-at-birth babies, Oedipal surprises, twins with amnesia, rich young men taking advantage of poor and innocent women, and lots and lots of women cat fighting and men dueling. Tango, like soap operas, connects our universally shared pain and drama. Tango not only is woven throughout Argentine history but threads through unexpected cultures around the world.

The king of Russian tango, Pyotr Leshchenko, was best known for his song "Serdtse" (Heart), which he sang in Russian but arranged as an Argentine tango. In the 1930s the Soviet Union considered the tango counterrevolutionary and banned his work, though fans still smuggled it into the country. He eventually died in a Romanian prison. Those present at his deathbed claimed his last words were lyrics from his famous song: "Friends, I am happy, for I will return to my fatherland! I am going away, but I leave you my heart."

However, it was Russia's next-door neighbor, Finland, where the tango really took hold. Finland had been part of Sweden until 1809, when the Russian empire claimed it until 1917. After

Finland gained independence, the Finns searched for a national identity and declared their country a minor-key nation. With this edict, Finns were able to differentiate themselves from Swedes—a major-key nation—and officially aligned themselves with music in the key of sadness. The tango allowed stoic, taciturn Finns to express their emotions and communicate with members of the opposite sex. And it offered them a social life during the long winters. Finland remade tango in its own image of music and dance, incorporating a polka-type beat. The Finnish and Argentine tangos are related somewhat the way second cousins are. This style wasn't exported, but it spread and entrenched itself inside the Nordic nation.

Another country where tango has long been a cultural phenomenon is Turkey. A friend had made me a CD of Old World tangos that I played over and over, as I tend to do with new CDs. I was particularly drawn to the songs of Turkish singer Seyyan Hanim. She had a high, haunting voice, and while the tango rhythm in her music was clear, the sensibility was pure Middle Eastern. I later learned that Turkey's first encounter with Western music was through the tango. The music, so fashionable in European capitals, was being played in nightclubs throughout Istanbul by the late 1920s, which showed the Turks' openness to Western culture.

The leader of the Turkish National Liberation movement, Mustafa Kemal Atatürk, ended the Ottoman dynasty and created the Republic of Turkey in 1923. Atatürk established a secular government and tried to steer the Turkish people toward influences from the West and Europe rather than from Muslim countries. Prior to this, no Turkish Muslim woman had been allowed on stage. Seyyan Hanim was a protégée of Kemal Atatürk, and he believed that her career could be symbolic of a new, more liberal nation. With his support, she became a popular singer and a symbol for emancipation of women. These days, Turkish politics still vacillates between secularists and Muslims: Culturally, whether to look to the East or the West is a constant argument. I suspect that dancing tango will be one of the true tests of secularism in Turkey.

After the set ended, I left the Russian and partnered with Allen. We noticed that one of the regular dancers was here without his regular partner. Like Domanitrix and her partner, they turned heads on the floor, but for different reasons. They were both tall and thin and excellent dancers. With their long legs complementing each other's perfectly, stepping in complicated patterns that seemed preternaturally graceful, they reminded me of compasses used in geometry classes, their legs swinging in arcs and circles around their bodies.

"Isn't he with a new partner?" I whispered to Allen.

"Yeah, I saw him with his original partner at a milonga earlier this week," Allen said. "They seemed to be having problems. Maybe even arguing."

"How did he find another tall, beautiful, excellent dancer so soon?" I asked.

"Maybe there's a number you can call," Allen said.

"Oh, look, he's training her," I said.

We watched as he spoke into the woman's ear and she nodded. They repeated the step he had just attempted.

"He's the Tango Whisperer," Allen said.

We both giggled and then I took the opportunity to ask Allen
about the woman he had been dating.

"Not going so well," he said.

"What happened?"

"Well, I started to notice that she was a little crazy," he said.
"So I started to back out, and she got crazier."

"What do you mean?" I asked.

"She sent me thirty-three text messages today," he said. "She
says she wants resolution."

He said it with a straight face, but I couldn't fight my smile.

"As Dario's prodigy, you should know all about resolution,"
I said.

When the tanda ended we went to the snack area. An elderly
gentleman opened a magnum of red wine and started pouring
the contents into people's cups. Claire and Peter joined us, and we
all watched people dance—the professionals, the obsessive ama-
teurs, the beginners and intermediates; the clutching and sliding,
the legs wrapping, axes being taken and new ones found.

We spotted one young couple who had no idea how to tango
and were slow dancing in the center of the floor.

"They must have read a listing for this somewhere and decided it would be a fun date," Allen said.

"Yeah, they have no idea what's going on here," said Claire.

They moved off, sat on a bench, and started necking in a passionate clutch. We laughed.

"You know, those two are the normal ones," I said. "They're on a date. Look at us."

"I met someone interesting the other night," Claire said. "I went to see a friend perform. Afterward a group of us went out for dinner. I was sitting next to a guy who had been out west, traveling on his motorcycle. He seemed kind of sweet but not wimpy. You know what I mean?"

"So what happened?" I asked.

"Nothing, really. Our mutual friend made him move to the other end of the table so he could chat with him. So I'm trying figure out where he goes and how to meet up with him again."

Peter spotted a gay tanguero and went over to ask him to dance. As I watched him, I felt a little sad because I realized that one day I would lose my dance buddies. It seemed inevitable. I knew these Friday nights would end: Claire and Peter and Allen, they'd find love interests and move on. There must be a term for that in the tango—melancholy from the inevitable passing of pleasure. Or feeling left in the dust.

"La Cumparsita" signaled the end of the evening, but we wanted to stay in the warm, dark room, muddling around in the oxbow while the river of activity flowed by outside. Slowly we changed shoes and went out into the New York nightlife; some events were waning and others just getting started. Cell phones snapped shut with a "Fuck you," and anxious men shuffled in long lines as they waited in the cold, hoping to enter a club where they'd heard models hang out. We passed among them, slightly smug in the knowledge that what they were seeking—the intimacy, the drama, the drugged feeling of falling in love— we had found. Even if just for a night, for a song, it would do for now. We stopped at a corner before heading in our separate directions.

"I used to live right over there," Peter said. "I can't believe I gave up that rent-controlled apartment. But I didn't think this city would get so expensive. Now I have to share a studio with a woman who sells flower essences," he said. "And she has two cats."

"That sounds cozy," I said.

He grimaced. "Way, way too cozy."

"Brooklyn is not that bad," Claire said. "You'd probably have better luck over there."

But Peter is one of those people who would rather, well, share a studio with a roommate and her pets than live in Brooklyn.

"I'm tired of this city," he answered. "The expense, the cold."

"It's not easy," I said. "That's true."

Claire and I parted from Allen and Peter in a quick exchange of kisses on cheeks before we went into the subway and waited for our train.

"I'm always hungry after a milonga, but I don't want to eat so late," I said.

"Bananas are good," Claire responded. "They have potassium and replenish your muscles."

She put a hand on a post and stretched her calves. I pointed one leg outward, subtly stretching it, then etched small circles with it, an embellishment termed a *lapiz*, or pencil.

"I wish everybody danced," Claire said. "Then, during lunch breaks, we'd all go out and tango under the trees."

"Embrace with total strangers, every day," I said. "You'd really get to know the best of a person."

"I feel like I'm starting to become friendlier with strangers," Claire said. "And even more affectionate with people I know."

"I think dancing helps us become more compassionate," I said.

The train roared into the station, and Claire sighed. "I love tango so much," she said. "You're so lucky you're going to Buenos Aires soon. Maybe you'll meet a handsome tanguero there."

I laughed. "I'm totally against any romance unless it lasts about three minutes and involves ochos."

But sometimes romance finds you in the most unlikely places.

CHAPTER 9

El Boleo, The Throw

I WANDERED ALONG the crooked, cobblestone streets of downtown Buenos Aires, jostled by the crowds on the narrow sidewalks and dodging the speeding cars. From this cityscape I searched for something the tango promised: a lessening of the grief, a segue from lost love into acceptance. In the full light of day it was business as usual for the Argentineans, but like a shadow, tango was always there; I passed by stores that sold dancing shoes and cafés where the occasional tango melody floated to the sidewalk. There's a term, *mufarse*, in the local dialect of Lunfardo, that carries the cadences and nuances of longing. (I had learned this term via Robert Farris Thompson and his book *Tango: The Art History of Love*.) Mufarse is the melancholic pleasure that comes from surviving the shock of heartbreak; it's relief that the worst has passed. This was the object of my search.

Though it seems unlikely anyone could find mufarse in a shopping mall, that's exactly where I went: through the labyrinth of stores and up elevators, following the nods and pointing fingers of security guards, until I found the famed Academia del Tango, marked by a phrase from tango composer Enrique Santos Discépolo scrawled across the wall: *"El tango es un pensamiento triste que hasta se puede bailar."* (The tango is a sad thought that you can dance.)

I entered the dance studio, where light beamed through tall glass windows, laminating the wood floors with a glossy sheen. Most of the students were women, but one of them told me this was unusual. The teacher, Augusto, seemed cheerful and enthusiastic. He had a round face, giving him a youthful appearance, which he countered by wearing thick-framed glasses. His posture and graceful, confident gestures made him handsome.

"Yesterday the class was all men," Augusto said. "But that doesn't matter. We will still have an excellent class, I assure you."

He demonstrated a *boleo*, whipping his leg energetically across himself, first in back, then in front of the leg that held his weight. He broke it down: "Cross your legs, knees are touching. Then let the free leg swing up, circle around behind you, and bring it in front of you."

I loved watching the boleo. It reminded me of a cat flicking its tail in warning.

Augusto watched us try it, then shook his head. "No, not yet. You don't have it," he exclaimed. "Let's try it with partners."

One of the few men led me, first on my right leg, then on my left. It didn't feel as poetic as it looked. I worried about damage to my knees as I swung them around. The follower is supposed to just let go and let her leg whip in response to the will of the leader.

"The boleo is an act of regret," Augusto told the class. "The leader is sending the follower away, but then in an instant he changes his mind and pulls her back to him. That moment is the boleo."

Sometimes the control given leaders bothered me, but at other times I liked their shouldering more of the responsibility when I was learning new steps. *Boleo* comes from the Spanish verb *bolear*, "to throw," but the movement is more like whipping.

After the lesson, I made my way through the crowds flowing down the narrow sidewalks of the city center, then broke away from the pedestrians to go to an afternoon milonga at the most famous tango hall in Buenos Aires, La Confitería Ideal. Built in the early 1900s, it had twenty-foot ceilings both up- and down-stairs, marble columns, and dark wood paneling. The hall was slightly smoky, the walls, floors, columns distressed and pati-naed. It was a perfect tango venue. A waiter, who looked as old as the building and had the stiff demeanor of a butler, pointed me up the marble staircase that wrapped around a wrought-iron elevator. The clientele at the afternoon milonga was a group of retirees and a sprinkling of tourists. A woman insisted on seating me at a table just to the side of the dance floor.

I ordered a *café cortado*, an espresso with a dollop of frothed milk on top. A classic tango played, and I thought about my ex-husband and grew melancholy. He was supposed to be here with me. We were supposed to go to the wedding together, take this trip together. Maybe the trip could have saved our marriage. I played over some of our conversations in my head and wondered if I had made mistakes. What if instead of saying, "I'm divorcing you," I had said, "Come home and let's work this out?" Maybe I was scared of his response. But what if I had said that? And what if he had come home? I wouldn't be sitting here alone right now. Big tears started slipping down my cheeks. I swabbed them with a coarse napkin and looked around the room.

The hostess had seated all the women in this section, while the men chatted among themselves at the tables near the head of the dance floor. I quickly learned why. At some milongas in Buenos Aires, men do not approach women to ask them to dance; rather, they sit across the room from them and make eye contact. If the woman does not avert her eyes, the man nods slightly, almost imperceptibly. If the woman nods back, then he approaches her table, or both stand and meet on the dance floor. The head motion, the subtle agreement, is known as a *cabeceo*, from the Spanish word for "head," *cabeza*. The verb *cabecer* means to move one's head, as if to nod; its noun form, *cabeceo*, is a tango invitation. The men are known as *cabeceros*. The cabeceo saves men from being rejected publicly, and it allows women to refuse gracefully.

Though a good solution, it did present a few problems. I encountered a man who seemed to stare at me, but he never made a gesture. I would catch his gaze, expectant, but the nod never came. At those times cabeceo seemed more like a staring match than an invitation. Was I missing the nod?

The cabeceros all seemed to have a repertoire of four to six dance moves they used over and over. They danced classic tango, from the early days before the nuevo moves like volcadas or the modern boleo were taught in classes. I liked this—they would not make a move that scared or surprised me. (The boleo, for example, still scared me a little. I hadn't been able to fully relax my leg and let it whip independently of my will.) If I didn't know a step that these cabeceros led, they gently walked me through it.

One man kept bending his leg and trying to get me to kick my foot in the space, spurring the air with a gancho, but he seemed so unsteady on his feet, I worried that if I flicked my heel where he wanted, we would both end up on the floor. Truthfully, I didn't fully understand what he was intending until he barked, "*Da me un ganchito!*" (Give me a little gancho!)

I flicked my foot with a slight jab. This seemed to satisfy him, and we danced on.

The afternoon at La Confitería Ideal had the clandestine feel of sitting in a bar during the day or making love on a weekday afternoon. Tango was an activity meant for nighttime, and only the most hardcore would cast away summer daylight hours here. The subtle agreements made with eyes and slight nods were mysterious, as if their coming together had been predetermined in another time and place.

After dancing with the cabeceos all afternoon, I left the dark, beautiful coffee shop and walked narrow sidewalks still bustling with foot traffic. I passed along city squares where trees arched over the walkways. I looked up and saw the forked branches of a jacaranda tree, stark and severe against the early twilight sky. On the sidewalk lavender petals littered the ground like pastel graffiti.

Early the next morning I flipped open my tango map and made my way to a shopping district, then into a small back alleyway where I followed a sign that read COMME IL FAUT. Inside the store, women perched on zebra-print love seats fumbled through piles of shoeboxes that spilled open onto the bloodred carpet. The jumble included all kinds of stilettos: red-heeled shoes with leopard print straps; bright turquoise ones with shiny silver straps across the toes; classic Chanel-style creamy beige with black swirls; rhinestone studs that shimmered as you moved them; black velvet with silver straps. The shoes were designed specifically for tango, with the heel aerodynamically angled for walking backward and, so dancers claim, the whole allowing for maximum foot articulation.

I sat down and told the saleswoman my size, adding, "Lowest heels possible, please."

I was informed that a two-inch stiletto was as low as they go. I tried on a few styles, walking in front of the mirror, complaining that the leopardskin didn't come in my size. I walked forward, pivoted, stepped backward, pushed my foot out to the side, rubbed it in a gentle circle against the floor, and brought it back in slowly. More women arrived, and I detected accents from England, the United States, and the Netherlands as we commented on the shoes, and the boxes got stacked until they teetered and toppled. Lids flew, and the saleswomen ran back and forth. I stood in front of the mirror, checking myself out in a pair of emerald green heels, and muttered, "I'm not sure they're practical."

"Don't even say that word," a woman responded, and everyone laughed.

Women piled up three and four boxes at the register. One young woman had five.

"I've never seen her in the same pair of shoes twice," her mother complained to the crowd.

"That's an exaggeration," the girl responded. "But I love these and they're so reasonable here."

After much consideration, I chose an elegant pair of two-inch black stilettos with a silver lamé strap. Not too showy, yet beautiful nevertheless, with the silver adding a hint of attitude. I noticed some of the women carrying Mimi Pinzón shopping bags: my next stop.

In Argentina I could live as if money didn't matter, so instead of marching to a subway and figuring out transfers, I hailed a cab. My luxury was possible due to an economic crisis triggered in 2001. After the government stopped making payments on its crushing foreign debt, banking institutions refused to loan the country any more money. People fearing the worst began withdrawing large sums of money from their bank accounts, turning pesos into dollars, sending them abroad, and causing a bank run. In order to stop this, the government imposed a limit on withdrawals. Economic activity froze, and street protests erupted around the country. The peso was devalued, creating hardships for the Argentineans but making the country cheap for foreigners. While the nation struggled to recover, Buenos Aires, the "Paris of the South," became *the* place to visit.

When I found out Katherine and Marcus were getting married in Uruguay, I pitched a magazine article that explored tango as a new economy in Buenos Aires. Argentina hoped tourism would help it recover from what it called the crisis, and tango was at the forefront of the plan. Bed-and-breakfasts offered tango classes; new dance schools opened, listing group and private classes. Some young tangueros even accompanied out-of-towners to milongas—these taxi dancers promised a good night of dancing for a small fee. Buenos Aires had become an affordable Mecca for tango, and even those visiting for other reasons often caught the bug and went home and learned the dance. While the crisis caused hardship for the nation, it bolstered tango's popularity in its birthplace, as well as internationally.

It was time to dress like a tango dancer. Racks of black clothing lined the walls in the dimly lit space in the Mimi Pinzón showroom, which was adorned only with a red crushed-velvet fainting couch. The designer, Viviana Laguzzi, had been a professional tango dancer before starting her business; her clothes had the stretch and sway dancers needed, and many had been created for stage performers. The saleswoman pulled out halter-top pant suits with slits from ankle to thigh and black, slinky dresses woven with gold lamé. They were flashy and shameless and meant to be ogled, but I opted out of the outrageous and bought black harem pants, which were in fashion. The material tucked up at the ankles so your heels didn't catch. I also got basic yet flattering black tops made of what felt like rayon and lycra fabrics, low cut and with some swing. I put on my dancing shoes, tried on a few black skirts, and decided on one that hung in jagged edges and another less opaque skirt with a serrated hem.

Many of these clothes were made with tourists in mind. The size large in Buenos Aires actually fits an American small or medium, and in a lot of clothing boutiques, trying on garments meant squeezing and zipper burns for the visitors and stifled giggles for the saleswomen. One of the great mysteries of Buenos Aires was how the women stayed so thin. *Portenos*, or residents of Buenos Aires, ate dinner at eleven o'clock at night. They disdained vegetables; if you could find a salad on a menu, it was usually uninspired—a pile of grated carrots dumped onto a plate, for example.

My friend Katherine and her Uruguayan fiancé, Marcus, had once invited me to a barbecue at their house in Brooklyn. Uruguayans are as carnivorous as the Argentineans. When I asked if I could bring something (I suggested a vegetable or salad), I was told not to bother. At the party it was as if a cow had exploded onto the grill—ribs and steaks and sausages; not a fresh, green piece of produce in sight. Marcus explained to me, "The chorizo is like the salad."

Steaks were eaten at all times of the day and night in Argentina. I saw construction workers in downtown Buenos Aires grilling short ribs for lunch on their cement-mixing wheelbarrow. It seemed that every meal was fattening. Breakfast almost always consisted of *medialunas* (semisweet croissants) and *dulce de leche* (caramel). I asked my friends Nola and Siobhan, who were traveling to the wedding with me, to please stab my hand with a fork if they saw me reaching for the dulce de leche at breakfast. But I couldn't resist and I worried my jeans would fit like sausage casings by the time I left. So what the hell did the local women eat to stay so thin?

I asked a few but they just shrugged, as if thinness were as effortless to them as speaking Spanish. I imagined they just didn't eat . . . at least not often and not much. And if they did, they'd better learn how to sew their own clothes. But this isn't natural or healthy, and an estimated one out of every ten women in Argentina had an eating disorder. This is the second-highest rate in the world, after Japan.

While I was there, the government was in the process of passing a law that required retail stores to stock clothing above a size eight. And as I observed, the Argentine equivalent to an eight is closer to an American size four or six. Apparently the law was meant to help stem the epidemic of anorexia and bulimia. The designers and store owners responded to the proposed law as if it were an act of colonialism—just because Americans are fat, why should we have to make our clothes bigger? While the spirit of the law was to help bigger-boned Argentineans, the burgeoning tourism industry would benefit, as well, when nonanorexic visitors could go into a dressing room without facing total humiliation.

Whether it was the stretchy fabrics or business acumen taking precedence over national pride, the designers at Mimi Pinzón made clothes that fit tango tourists. The prices were at most a third of what they would have been in the States. My shopping bags rubbing against one another, I should have felt a little guilty for taking advantage of the economic crisis. But quite selfishly, as I hailed a taxicab, I was mostly thinking, Now that I'm going to look like a dancer, I need to know how to dance.

CHAPTER 10

El Molinete, The Wheel

MY TEACHER, WHO was from the Academy of Tango, lived in a small apartment bare of furnishings except for a lone chair in the living room, to which he ushered me so I could change my shoes. Augusto was also a performer, and I noticed that foot swipes ran across the walls and a few scuff marks even dotted the ceiling.

"I live with my partner," he said. "We practice here."

He asked me what I wanted to work on.

"I want my hips to pivot like well-oiled hinges," I said.

"*Que?*" he asked.

"Okay, how about the *molinete,*" I answered.

Molinete means "wheel" or "windmill." The woman steps in a grapevine pattern, crossing herself side, back, and forth around the man while he pivots in circles; he continues to pivot on his axis, and she moves in a tight triangle around him. She must follow his chest, not his legs, keeping her chest aligned with his.

"You are knotting yourself up with your partner," Augusto said. "It is how do you say, a paradox. You're twisting together. Think of it as two snakes fighting."

Though I prepared myself for serpentine knots, Augusto insisted that we start with *los elementales* (the basics), so we began with the embrace.

"I'm not your great-aunt, hold me like you mean it," he instructed. He pulled me closer and secured an arm around my waist. "Now when I turn my chest, you have to follow that. Keep your axis, twist more at your waist, sink into the floor, and now push off it to step away."

It wasn't quite as brutal as my first private lesson in New York. Augusto lived the tango and treated his talent as a gift to share. His optimism was infectious, and I took to his tango wisdom like a groupie.

"Remember, the tango is a conversation, never an argument," he told me. "It always flows smoothly." He spun on his axis, and I worked to catch up with him, chest to chest, stepping around him, orbiting a center of gravity. I twisted at the waist, separating my upper and lower body. I tried to not put weight on him so he was free to turn, and we circled around each other in centrifugal motion until we grew dizzy, then stopped and spun the other way.

Toward the end of the lesson he ceased his instruction and just danced with me.

"Close your eyes," he said.

He felt sublime. The confidence that he transferred to me

made me feel safe and cared-for and valued. By just simply walking and turning, stopping and starting, he led me to places I hadn't been before. There's an expression in tango, "*La lleva como dormida*," which means "He leads her as asleep." This is when the follower trusts her leader so completely that she relaxes fully, closes her eyes, and reaches a slightly somnambulant dreamlike state.

While dancing this way with Augusto, I became acutely aware of the scent of his neck, the soothing energy radiating from his chest, his breath occasionally brushing my face. I remembered how good it felt to fall asleep with a man. To feel his skin against the length of my body, the weight of his arms around me, and to hear his breathing change, slow down and then deepen, as he fell asleep. I felt myself start to want that in a way that punctured my protective bubble, my resolution that tango would be enough.

In that bare, stark room with the ceiling and walls marked and scratched with practice steps, in a place where only tango mattered, I realized the paradox of the molinete: that it was possible to experience the lingering sadness of past heartbreak and the tingle of future romance at the same time.

"Have you been to a milonga yet?" he asked.

"I'm going to one tonight," I told him. "In San Telmo."

"Perfect," he said.

San Telmo is in the southern section of the city, and at times the scents of the port—rusted anchors, diesel fumes, exposed mud, and murky waters—wafted by. The cobblestone streets and the buildings with their ornate ironwork had an Old World charm. Many of the areas, though, were run down, and the streetlights illuminated the shabbiness of the well-worn community. I wondered about being dropped here by myself at 11:00 P.M. but went ahead and stepped out of the cab. Milonga Gay was on the second floor of a dark building. Peter had told me that this was the best milonga in town—although his opinion was, of course, biased. (I also wanted to include gay tourism as another angle for the article I was writing.)

Before going in I made a quick detour and bought some gum in the event I danced that night. Just as I returned to the door and pressed the buzzer, I noticed a man who also had arrived for the milonga. We smiled at each other. He was about my height and had dark, curly hair and brown eyes that turned down slightly at the corners.

"*¿Hablas inglés?*" he asked.

"*Claro que sí,*" I said. "Rather, most certainly."

"This is kind of an out-of-the-way place," he said. "Do you dance tango?"

"I've been learning," I said.

I assumed that Josh was gay, so without hesitation I invited myself to join him. He offered to buy me a drink. I asked for a glass of red wine, and he ordered a sparkling water for himself. The walls had been painted dark red, and strings of white lights reflecting off small mirrors gave the room a shabby-chic glamour. The music switched from classic heartbreak tango to jazzy and upbeat nuevo tango. The couples varied: There were women with women and a few mixed-gender couples, but mostly men danced with men—and they were excellent dancers. They turned and ganchoed and boleoed, whipping, kicking, executing their steps with precision and clarity of intent. They followed the line of dance, or the circular flow of the couples around the dance floor, five-o'clock-shadowed cheek to cheek.

"My tango teacher told me I had to be here tonight. It was nonnegotiable" Josh explained to me. "She should be here soon. So you want to dance?"

I accepted, though I approached the floor with a little apprehension, as the dancers were so advanced. I followed Josh as he made his way to the floor, where he stopped and faced me. We embraced—not close, but open. I looked into his chiseled face, his kind brown eyes, and smiled. He started stepping the basic and I knew right away that this was going to be exceptionally bad. He not only didn't maneuver the basic steps securely, but he also didn't hold his arms in a way that made a connection possible. Where our hands joined, he pumped his arm up and down and swung it all over the place. The floor was crowded, and he just stood there, motionless, waiting for a place for us to fit on the dance floor, then he sort of run-dragged me to that spot and started the hand pumping once again.

"Have you learned the rock step yet?" I asked him.

"The what?" he yelled over the music.

"It's if you get stuck and can't move, you sort of rock back and forth from front foot to back foot, so you keep dancing, then when you see an opening, you dance toward it and join the line of dance again."

"Oh, like this?" he asked.

We practiced it, and I noticed members of the crowd watching us with bemused curiosity. When the song ended, I hurried back to my seat and Josh followed. I hoped he hadn't yet learned that you normally dance for three songs. While we sat together, I found out a piece of his story. He had an MBA and had worked in San Diego, investigating foreclosures. He had recently quit his job and taken off for South America to spend a year traveling. He was staying at a youth hostel in the center of town—if he was going to have the experience of backpacking, he was going to go all the way. I invited him to have dinner with me at a tango show I was writing about for my article. Later in our conversation, it came out that he was straight.

When I was leaving he walked me out and opened the taxi door for me. On the way to my hotel, I realized that I had just asked a man out on a date.

I waited for Josh in the hotel restaurant, at a table at the edge of the parquet floor where the dancers would perform. He arrived carrying a large bouquet of yellow flowers. I was a little embarrassed but appreciated the gesture. The waiter took the flowers for us, and Josh ordered a carbonated water. Almost immediately, he told me, "I'm in AA and don't drink."

Coming from a large, Irish Catholic family that's part of a larger Irish Catholic community, I was very familiar with the program. When I was a child, "on the wagon" or "off the wagon" had been two of the most common explanations for sudden changes in adult behavior.

"When did you quit?" I asked. "Was it because of your divorce?"

"No, I divorced three years after I quit drinking," he said. "My wife found a new guy with a drug problem. I thought my life was horrible at that point and really felt sorry for myself . . . because of my divorce and knowing that I couldn't drink. But they were the best possible things for me. Here I am."

"Why South America?" I asked.

"I was always obsessed with money," he said. "I got a sense of power from it—just knowing I had it. But I realized, or actually my sponsor asked me one day, who I was living my life for. I didn't know. I had always wanted to come to South America, so I'm spending a year down here."

When I worked seasonal jobs in Alaska, I escaped the long winters by going to Latin America. I hiked the Inca Trail and climbed a mountain in the Cordilleras Blancas. I visited a jungle along the Amazon, worked in an orphanage in the swampy rain forest of Guatemala, hitchhiked through Mexico, and danced in Cuba.

"I need to quit my life of travel and adventure and find a steady job and make some money," I told him. "As a freelancer, I live hand to mouth and on the brink of financial disaster all the time. But it's hard to change. Just knowing you have this year ahead of you makes me so envious."

"You can be my adventure adviser and I'll be your financial adviser," he said. "Before I went into that milonga, I circled the block because I was so nervous. It's strange we arrived at the exact same time. It makes me think we met for a reason."

"I had gone to buy a pack of gum," I said. "If I had headed straight in, we wouldn't have met. And as your adventure adviser, I suggest that you climb a mountain in South America."

"I'll think about that," he said.

From what I knew about AA, most people there had hit rock bottom. They'd lost everything—job, family, and home. They were left to wallow in the mire of shame and self-disgust, then had to pick themselves back up and crawl out of the hole. From this void, people can be reborn into a better life than what they ever imagined. Divorce also feels like hitting rock bottom: You are stuck in the nastiest, worst emotions a person can feel. You have to believe that things will get better and surrender to the fact that your life is going to be very different from how you imagined it. But this vital lesson doesn't come easy, and maybe a tango-dancing sponsor was what I needed.

We studied our menus.

"So I guess the smart choice here is beef?" I mused.

"Usually a safe bet," he said.

We ordered and then the lights dimmed, the music started, and the performers came out, the leader in a dark suit and the follower in a slinky red dress with a long slit that showed off her thigh. They danced the history of tango. It was provocative, with gestures that suggested flirtatious banter and the push and pull of seduction. They kicked and spun, then separated, but stayed connected; their steps were a call and response, a question and answer; and then a truce. The braggadocio turned to sadness and they danced closely, forehead to forehead, embracing each other as if their lives depended on it.

MY FRIENDS AND fellow wedding guests Nola and Siobhan had arrived in Buenos Aires for some sightseeing, late-night steak dinners, and wine drinking before we all left for the wedding in Montevideo. On Sunday morning Josh came by our guesthouse and escorted us to the antiques fair in San Telmo. We wandered among booths where hawkers displayed vintage chain-link purses, glass seltzer bottles in hues of blue and purple, cut-crystal lamps, ornate vases, silver jewelry, mirrors in gilded frames, tango records, and huge dusters made of ostrich feathers. Between the wares, performers danced the tango, with hats set out for tips. We all wanted to peruse different tables at different paces, so we agreed to split up and meet up later in the day.

Josh and I stayed together and watched raven-haired beauties in red dresses dance with brown-eyed men in white shirts and black pants. I had to be dragged from the group of men squeezing their bandoneóns.

"I need an empanada," I said.

"Come on," Josh said. "I know a place."

We made our way through the crowds until we found the small storefront that smelled of baking bread.

"All I have is a big bill," I said.

"Okay, I'll pay," Josh said.

"Thank you," I said and kissed his cheek.

"What have I gotten myself into?" he answered.

We ordered empanadas made with gorgonzola cheese, and the man put them on a wood paddle and slid them into the oven. Josh ate his quickly and I wasn't quite finished when he said, "I'm going to have to go. I have a meeting. But I wanted to tell you something. You hurt my feelings the other night."

"Why?" I asked.

"When you got into the cab and rode away, you didn't look back," he said.

"Well, I'm glad you mentioned that," I answered. "Because I would have just bellied up to the empanada bar. Now I'm going to look back."

He laughed, kissed me quickly, and started walking down the street. I stepped outside and yelled, "See, I'm looking."

He just waved his arm, refusing to turn his head.

The previous night, just before I had gotten out of the cab, he'd kissed my cheek and said, "Good night, beautiful." Despite all the de rigueur stares and whistles and comments that Argentinean men directed at women walking down the streets, this casual comment seemed flip and untrue. I felt bruised by it, as though Josh had lied to me or said something he thought he should say that was clearly an untruth. So I hadn't turned as the taxi drove off.

Whenever I looked in the mirror, I saw only my imperfections — the crow's feet around my eyes, the sun spot on a cheek, the slight crevices forming in my upper lip, the small gaps between my teeth. Of course my husband wanted to be with another woman. Since he wasn't around to tell me why he fell out of love with me, I had been searching for reasons on my face and body.

After I finished eating, I wandered the marketplace until I

came to a display of photographs of tango dancers. These were the equivalent of a picture of the Statue of Liberty for tourists in New York, but still I wanted to get one or two for my apartment. Many showed people striking dramatic poses in the middle of the street, the men's hair slicked back and the women's pulled tightly in a bun. Even the clothes and cityscape were fraught with drama and passion: fishnet stockings, stilettos, the narrow, shaded streets of Buenos Aires.

I selected one that showed a couple in a close embrace. They seemed to be at home; their features were backlit by a large window, so only their silhouettes could be seen. They stood just inches apart, the connection between them palpable. The second one was of a couple posing at Confitería Ideal. They looked glamorous, nothing like my cabeceros with their scratchy, bearded cheeks and the scent of their worn wool clothing.

I then dug out my notepad and headed to Lugar Gay, a guesthouse that catered exclusively to men, located right off the central plaza. I was going to watch the afternoon tango lessons and conduct a few interviews for my article. The door opened to a spiral staircase that wound its way up to a comfortable sitting room. A handsome young man wearing a white tank top greeted me. He introduced himself as Javier and offered to make me a coffee.

"Water would be great," I said. "What's your job here?"

"*Chico de la casa*," he said. He handed me a cold glass of water.

"The houseboy, huh?" I asked. "Can women stay here?"

"I'm sorry," he said. "If it were up to me you could. But it's not allowed."

I looked up and noticed a print of a famous photograph hanging in the hallway. It was a black-and-white vintage shot of hundreds of men in the tango embrace. Javier introduced me to Arturo, an architect who taught the history of architecture at a university in Buenos Aires and gave tours of the city to guests staying at Lugar Gay. Arturo was short, with broad shoulders and a kind, earnest face. I liked him immediately. We sat in the living room while he told me about the photo and the neighborhood.

Along with La Boca, San Telmo was one of two southern areas of the city that claimed to be the birthplace of tango. Home to Buenos Aires's aristocrats during the time known as *epoca de las rosas*, San Telmo flourished for ten years, until yellow fever swept through it in the late 1800s. The wealthy, afraid of disease, left the southern part of the city. This flight left a lot of empty mansions, which were divided into small flats for newly arriving immigrants.

"There were so many more men than women arriving here that they had to dance together," Arturo said. "Most of the women who danced tango back then were prostitutes." He explained that although the white slave trade started around 1890, the biggest trafficker, the Zwi Migdal Society, was founded in 1906. Members of this organization of Jewish gangsters would travel through Eastern Europe in search of girls. When they found young women in shtetels, many of them living in poverty and in fear of anti-Semitic pogroms, the girls readily accepted their proposals of marriage and the opportunity for a better life in Argentina. The young women packed their bags, expecting domestic happiness in Buenos Aires. Instead, they found themselves being forced to work the brothels. These Yiddish-speaking prostitutes were known as Polacas.

I asked Arturo what happened to the Africans in Argentina. At one point, in the 1700s, they made up almost 50 percent of the population. Now if you saw a person of color in Buenos Aires, you could bet he or she was a visitor.

"I'm not entirely sure," he said. "That's a really shadowy part of our history. When the European immigration peaked in the 1880s, the people in power wanted a white country and sold the blacks, shipped them away, or sent them to fight the border wars with Brazil. There's still a strong African culture in Uruguay, so some historians think they were merely transported across the Río de la Plata. During carnival over there, you can still see the Candombe, the Afro-Uruguayan drummers and dancers. Believe it or not, some scholars claim that this is the precursor to the tango."

We walked back through the guesthouse, paused at the photo, and looked at the smiling men clutching each other. I thanked Arturo for the interview, and Javier showed me to the rooftop, where a tango lesson was taking place. We wound our way through an area filled with chaise longues. Handsome men sunbathed naked.

"You sure I can't stay here?" I joked with Javier.

"I'm sorry," he said, smiling. "House rules."

The lesson had already started, and I sat on the side and watched. As usual, some dancers were more advanced than others. The teacher walked with a particularly erect back, snapping his fingers to the beat. A pair of men, who I assumed were a couple because they sort of resembled each other, followed him with serious expressions; an Asian man walked with a slight smile; a large, blond dancer, who probably hailed from northern Europe or Australia, stepped with his arms stiff at his side. A few didn't know tango but seemed to have a strong physical awareness and corrected themselves easily, while others had to be shown a technique over and over. Boyfriends bickered; strangers were more polite to each other. All in all not so different from the hetero crowd.

The existence of this place was very significant in terms of Argentina's history. The country's long-standing dictatorship, which lasted until 1983, considered anything different subversive. Though there were no formal laws discriminating against homosexuals, an Edict Against Public Dancing punished any proprietor who "allowed men to dance together." This law was enforced until about 1995. Individuals who were arrested could be held by police for up to thirty days and fined.

Arturo had told me that since the economic crisis of 2001, Argentina has been trying to lure gay travelers to Buenos Aires. A gay tourist map highlighted guesthouses and queer bars, and sales presentations were made at gay travel symposiums. In 2002 the city council passed a measure recognizing same-sex civil unions and extending health insurance and pension rights to same-sex partners. Now Buenos Aires rivals Rio de Janeiro as *the* place to go for gay men.

When the tango lesson ended, I caught up with the teacher for a brief interview. Marcos was known as the man who started gay tango. Peter had told me all about him. Marcos, who had danced for the Broadway musical *Forever Tango*, told me that gay tango wasn't a deliberate movement; it just happened.

"One night I was dancing with a man," he said. "Then the next time, another couple of gay men joined us. And so on. Now we have lessons and a milonga. Can I help you with anything else?" he asked. He was packing up his dance shoes.

I had a moment when I could have blurted out, "Peter really likes you." But I wasn't entirely sure who Peter had slept with and pissed off, so I figured that tossing his name around might not be a good idea. I just tucked away my notebook, and Javier showed me out.

The antiques fair had ended, and the streets were empty except for strewn paper and other debris. The frenzy had passed, and soon the plaza would go back to being a place where young couples met to hold hands and kiss, the elderly gathered to argue politics and soccer, and the antiques, the tango, the history of the well-worn ports would lie dormant until Sunday came around again.

A tango class was in progress in the small studio just off the garden at my pension. The couples worked on steps as the music floated over the silhouettes of broad tropical leaves clustered against the stone walls. While waiting for Josh, I sat outside in the shadows of the palm fronds and thought about my fantasy, the one in which I'd visually erased my husband and then was walking down a hallway toward a patio where I danced tango in the arms of a man who loved me. Actuality, of course, fell short of my fantasy. Josh didn't love me, and he certainly was not going to dance a life-changing tango. But he was perfect for right then.

I heard the bell ring, the manager let Josh in, and as he entered the garden, he said, "Sorry I'm late. The subway stalled for a dog on the track."

We left for a nearby restaurant. Although the food and wine in Buenos Aires are excellent and inexpensive, the service is so slow that even a casual dinner can be a four-hour affair. As well, people don't eat until very late, so while we waited I passed from hungry to cranky to an almost giddy state by the time any food made it to our table. All the while, Josh and I joked about the service.

"Do you think she heard us when we ordered the water?" Josh asked.

"Hard to say," I answered. "Have we ordered food yet? We might need to start stalking her. I think I saw her go into the back."

"Bread, even just a piece of bread," he begged.

The trendy restaurant in the "Soho" part of the city grew increasingly crowded and noisy. We finally hailed the waitress and cajoled her into taking our order. We decided on two types of steaks that we'd share. Looking around the crowded room, Josh asked me, "Do you ever take yourself out to dinner? Just go to a restaurant like this and sit alone?"

"No," I said. "It's a social thing for me. I eat lunch out by myself sometimes, but I always sit at counters and read."

"My sponsor made me do that as an exercise," he said. "He told me that I needed to go sit at a table by myself in a crowded restaurant until I realized I had everything I needed within myself."

"I'd rather just eat at home and contemplate that," I said.

"Well, we'll have to work on that," Josh said. "Why do you think I should climb a mountain?"

"I don't know," I said. "It changes you. I did it in Peru and then again in Northern California. They were very different experiences. I suffered so much in Peru. My head pounded, my legs shook. At base camp I couldn't sleep or eat, from the altitude. All around us the air was filled with the rumblings of glaciers calving, and the smell of ice surrounded our tents. But when we descended and the air thickened, I have never been so grateful for oxygen and green grass. I guess that's one of the lessons of mountain climbing: gratitude. And the harder you push yourself, the more you learn how much suffering you can take. It's always more than you imagined."

"I've been thinking about it," he said. "I'm heading to Chile soon, and I think I'll try it."

Our steaks finally came, and as we ate, Josh looked directly into my eyes and said, "I feel like dancing some tango tonight."

We went to a milonga at Salon Canning, a venue with lots of light, colorful paintings of couples dancing, and a large dance floor made of blond wood. Inwardly I groaned. We would be seen by everyone under the bright lights. Just then a group of "alpha" tango dancers arrived. They were dressed in black silk and satin, the men in polished dance shoes, the women in high heels with iridescent bands of gold and silver running through them. With their erect posture and haughty demeanor, they hit the dance floor and put on a show for the small crowd. They embellished the simplest of steps, snapped their legs when they pivoted, dragged their feet over the ground when they stepped.

"You ready?" Josh asked.

I took a deep breath. "Why not," I said.

We went onto the floor, and I had to admit, Josh's embrace had improved. He no longer pumped his arms wildly. I felt a little more secure following him, but just a little. As we started the basic I thought he was moving me into a forward ocho, but he wasn't. So we bumped knees. Then we tried again and tangled feet. I didn't want everyone watching this, so I pulled him off the floor.

"Hey, what are you doing?" he asked.

"Let's work this out," I said. "I'm not sure what you're leading."

"Just let me lead and it will be fine," he said. "You need to surrender."

"Okay," I agreed.

We went back onto the dance floor.

"I think that was our first fight," Josh said. "It was cute."

"Let's just stick with the basic," I said.

We made our way around the dance floor, and I noticed that the alpha dancers had taken their seats. A chef had just stepped out of the kitchen and was dancing with a plump, elderly lady. It must have been slow back in the kitchen. I hoped they drew the attention sufficiently away from us.

"You need to stop worrying about what people think," Josh said. "In fact, as soon as we get in front of that table, I'm going to bust out my fanciest move." He motioned to the table occupied by the dancers.

"Please, no," I said. I pictured a moment of extreme humiliation. This was my perfect nightmare—appearing very bad at something right in front of people who were excellent at it. They would know just how inadequate I was.

"Oh yeah, you're in for a real surprise," he said.

I burst out in nervous laughter. He smiled back at me—not backing down, ready to teach me something. Ready to sponsor me in surrender.

I panicked as we moved toward the alphas and I glimpsed their stilettos, their perfect hair, the gleam of their black clothing. Oh, God, no, I thought. And then mercifully the song ended before Josh attempted any fancy moves.

When we left the place, a warm breeze was blowing outside. Josh wanted me to stand out of the wind while he waved down a taxi. We tucked ourselves into a storefront, and he kissed me—not a peck but a full lingering one on my lips. It was my first kiss since my husband left. I had wondered about this moment. Would I cry? Would I miss him? Would it be too soon? Josh's lips felt thin as he pressed them against mine. It wasn't a generous, life-altering kiss, but it was nice. And I didn't feel sad or miss my husband. Not right then, not at all.

We decided to go to another milonga, this one outdoors, because I wanted to see as much as I could for the article. At La Calesita tangueros danced around a central palm tree illuminated with strings of colorful lights. The smell of grilling meat filled the air, and people sitting around tables shared bottles of red wine. Josh and I bumped our way around the dance floor. I had decided that spending time with him was more important than a good dancing experience. I closed my eyes — rather tightly so I didn't have to witness the faces of the dancers we bumped into — and let him lead.

After a few songs we found a table. Josh bought me a glass of wine and himself sparkling water. "Look, the Southern Cross," he said, pointing to the sky.

By looking up at the stars just then, I felt a synesthesia: all the senses experiencing different things — the smell of fire, the tang of red wine, the blur of distant constellations, the feel of Josh's skin as we held hands, and the sounds of tango music — yet coming together to create a singular sensation. Gently squeezing Josh's hand, I realized that this was mufarse, the shiver of pleasure, the gentle melancholy. I had survived heartbreak.

CHAPTER 11

El Candombe, Afro-Uruguayan Music and Dance

ON THE OUTSKIRTS of Montevideo, bright sprays of magenta bougainvillea cascaded over garden walls. Toward the city center, colonial buildings with wrought-iron balconies and French doors flanked the steep and winding cobblestone streets that led to a long promenade separating the city from the Río de la Plata. People gathered and played soccer, strolled, sat and visited, or whispered and kissed one another along the promenade wall.

My friend Siobhan and I decided to go running to try and work off the dulce de leche we had been eating. We joked about finding dates to the wedding while we were out.

"I'm so tired of being at the singles table," Siobhan complained.

"I don't even want to think about it," I said.

"How'd you leave it with Josh?" she asked.

"I don't know," I said. "He just started his year of traveling in Latin America. And I can't join him, so I guess we're going to let it go and see what happens."

"Hey, look, a soccer game. Should we take them on?"

"If they lost to a couple of gringas they'd have to turn in their Uruguayan passports."

"We could blackmail them into being our dates tonight."

But we continued jogging along the river, then the color of weak coffee; crisp winds blew from the south, but the sun shone and the air had a dry crackle to it.

I had noticed, we had all noticed, in fact, that the bride, Katherine, was pregnant. In the hotel lobby, she stood with a hand on her belly and smiled when our gaze hesitated at her stomach.

"We didn't want to tell anyone until we were safely past three months," she said.

As we jogged, Siobhan mentioned the pregnancy and we picked up our pace. We weren't exactly jealous of the marriage or child, but it did make us feel left behind. Like other women who found themselves single and nearing forty, we just kind of wondered how our lives had turned out like this. A family was something we had just assumed would happen.

My grandparents didn't divorce. In heated moments my parents still threaten each other with it, but they would never divorce. Statistically speaking, I should have had a much more successful marriage because of that. Though I certainly wasn't the first person in my extended family to divorce. On my mother's side, two of my aunts and one uncle divorced. My mother's family was stoic and didn't discuss personal matters, so I didn't really know the particulars when they happened. Later I learned that my aunt's husband had been cheating on her when she was pregnant, and she had left him. Another aunt married at the age of eighteen to get out of her house; years later she became a feminist, found a better-paying job, divorced her husband, and put herself through college.

My uncle was an emotionally volatile Vietnam vet. A few years after his divorce he got drunk at a Thanksgiving dinner and yelled at me, "A writer? You'll never be a writer! You know what it's like to shoot a pregnant woman? A soldier remembers." I could just imagine why that marriage ended. But women's liberation and the upheaval of war never really changed my mother — she loved the conservative 1950s.

She used to tell my siblings and me that as a child she had wanted to be a Mouseketeer or a nun. When she was in a good mood and singing, she related the Mouseketeer dream to us; when she was angry with us, she started muttering about how she should have been a nun. While she claimed to dream of being a housewife and staying at home to raise her five unruly children, in reality she taught full time and went to school at night to get her master's degree and then sixty hours toward her Ph.D. She handled the family's finances and gave my father a weekly allowance. An overachiever, she implemented progressive reading programs in the troubled Kansas City public school system. All the while, she talked — without irony — about how she hoped I would marry a Catholic doctor and live the life of a housewife.

"Doctors' wives even have nice maternity clothes," she once told me. Quite an enticement for a high school girl.

In fact, she knew of a Catholic college in Nebraska that was attached to a medical school. All I had to do was get accepted to the school, go to the Christian gatherings, and stay a virgin until my wedding night. I defied my mother by going to a public university and paying my own way by working as a waitress so she couldn't do anything about it. Back then I dated guys in alternative rock 'n' roll bands; then I took off for Alaska, where I shacked up with a mountain climber for six years. I left Alaska—and the relationship—for graduate school in New York City.

Over the years, my mother and I came to forgive each other, and by the time I married she was so thrilled that she and my father went out and took salsa-dancing lessons for the wedding reception.

My parents knew how to dance. They didn't dress up and go out ballroom dancing, but they surprised the family at times. Every year on St. Patrick's Day our mostly Irish American parish had a party that included an Irish jig competition, and my parents frequently won. The prize was a live piglet—a hold over, I guess, from the old country. They brought it home and let us chase it around the backyard for a few days before selling it to a farm. At father-daughter high school dances, my father took me on the floor and spun and twirled me all night. I loved it.

I didn't know the origins of my father's dancing prowess until one night when we were watching the film *Dirty Dancing* on television. Patrick Swayze plays a dance instructor at a Catskills resort and demonstrates the dark art of Latin dance to the privileged clientele. After hours the employees shimmy, shake, and sweat all over each other. "Baby," the daughter of a guest, falls in love with this forbidden dancing, and also with the hunky bad boy, Swayze. For the big finale, Swayze pulls her out of the crowd and makes her show her stuff to the audience of her parents and their friends, with the now famous line "Nobody puts Baby in a corner." My father cried during this scene. He has wept during many films, but *Dirty Dancing*?

We finally pried the reason out of him. When working as a caddy at a golf course over his summer vacations, part of my father's duties was to dance with the clients' daughters. So every night he had to scrub up and swing or square dance with the rich girls.

"Holy crap. Dad was a taxi dancer," I remember commenting.

"Dad was Patrick Swayze," my sister added.

The wedding was held just outside of town at an old estancia. Palm trees surrounded a swimming pool and open lawn area, where a stage had been set up for the ceremony. Katherine looked beautiful in a Christian Dior dress and a retro hairstyle of tight waves against her head. Marcus looked handsome in his suit, but he was a shy person and the fear in his eyes betrayed discomfort over getting this sort of attention. The ritual itself passed quickly. Though Katherine was baptized Catholic, she had agreed to a Jewish wedding for Marcus's sake. A rabbi sang much of the ceremony. My heels sank into the soft ground, and I arched my neck to see the stage.

Immediately following the ceremony, wine was served. We paced ourselves because we heard rumors that the reception would go until morning. As we negotiated the seating, a chorus of "singles table" comments erupted. One woman, from Los Angeles, was also going through a divorce.

"So why aren't you at the singles table?" I asked her. "Is there a special table for those whose divorces aren't final yet? Technically, I am just separated."

"Why am I not at your table?" another guest asked. "I'm not married."

"You're at the long-term-committed-relationship table," I said.

"No, more like the afraid-of-commitment table," she answered.

Despite the stigma, everyone wanted to be seated with us because my single "sisters," Nola and Siobhan, danced. Really danced. And that's what creates the epicenter of a good party. Nola and Siobhan have been known to take on whole armies of young girls in dance competitions at weddings, going move for move with the youngsters and emerging victorious. That was to seventies music. When songs from the eighties started, people just stepped back. As for Latin rhythms, I could keep the party going.

That night everyone danced. The men gathered around Marcus and bounced in a football-like huddle. I led Katherine in a salsa, then danced with some of her mother's friends while the crowd jostled and jumped in celebration. As is the custom in Uruguay, the guests dance for a set before the first course was served. Then more music and dancing, followed by another course. No beef appeared on the menu at all. Marcus explained: "We eat meat every day. This a special occasion, so we have chicken."

We had one especially charming man at our table, and Siobhan and I joked that Katherine and Marcus had rented him for the evening. He engaged us all in conversation, made sure we had plenty of water and wine, and at one point reached over for a bug making its way to a woman's plate, saying, "Oh, excuse me, but this is mine." He picked it up, examined it, then tossed it from the table.

When it came time to throw the bridal bouquet, Katherine begged me to get Siobhan and Nola out there on the floor.

"Didn't you ask them already?" I asked.

"They won't budge," she said.

So I rallied them, and eventually, amid comments like "Oh, for Christ's sake," we all marched out. We stood toward the back, feet planted and arms dangling at our sides. Some young Uruguayan women lurched forward, and after a tussle, one caught the flowers. She tapped a little victory dance and waved them at her boyfriend.

A while later Katherine's sister-in-law approached me, a little concerned because Siobhan wasn't dancing. I checked on her. She needed water. She was getting tired. A few others seemed to be fading, plopping down at the tables, waving off the waiters serving wine. But then we heard live drumming and people were instantly revitalized.

An Afro-Uruguayan candombe band headed for the party,

led by two black beauties wearing nothing but tasseled pasties covering their nipples, a G-string, and high heels. And they had bodies—not skinny little bodies but curves that didn't stop: thin waists leading to mounded butts, and large, full breasts so firm they didn't jiggle despite the rapid hip and shoulder shakes. I spotted a boy watching them with his mouth literally open, eyes wide and unblinking. The dancers were followed by a procession of drummers tapping, hitting, beating, stroking different sizes of instruments; some drums gave off mellow tones, others boomed. The crowd followed them in a conga line, men and women trying to swivel their hips and keep the beat. Katherine's mom nudged me. "C'mon, you can move your hips like that. I've seen you."

I tried, but keeping up with those dancers gave me a cramp. I knew who could: my ex-husband. He would have been the one to watch during the drumming. I hadn't thought about him much that day, even though it was his birthday. I tried not to imagine him celebrating with his new girlfriend, his new family, but suddenly I felt my good mood drain from me. My eyes started to sting as I fought back tears.

Just then Katherine grabbed me and pulled me into the dancing crowd. Both of us shook our hips in time to the music, and soon I was laughing. The group around us felt like a hive buzzing— we had become a single entity. The candombe dancers were the queen bees, leading us in the language of the drummers. I didn't know if it was because of an undercurrent of African culture, or the way dancing puts you into your body and lets you transcend it at the same time, but the Afro-Uruguayan music started to feel like a prayer. In the history of the world, an awful lot of prayers have gone unanswered, yet people don't stop praying. If it is done with enough passion and enough faith, the prayer starts to become the answer to itself. As we all danced, I felt a crackling charge emanating from the crowd, and in place of sadness, I was filled with the spirit of joy.

CHAPTER 12

La Arrastrada, The Sweep

WHEN I RETURNED home from Buenos Aires, I opened the envelope from my lawyer and read over the black-and-white photocopy of my divorce decree. I would now have to check the "divorced" box on customs forms when I traveled abroad. Although belonging to this category might cause me pain, or shame or sadness, the vintage term *divorcée* implied a lasciviousness that made me smile. I decided to embrace it and referred to myself as "A Divorcée."

I redecorated my bedroom, divorcée style. I painted it lavender, then added two bedside tables, each with a lamp with red paper shades. I shifted my bureau between the two windows and placed on it an off-white ceramic pitcher with a dozen red roses. I painted my old wooden armoire eggshell; I covered the old, smoky mirrors with muted turquoise fabric and tacked peacock feathers onto them. As a finishing touch I framed the photos

of tango-dancing couples and hung them on the wall opposite my bed. At night I would admire the sensual glow of red
light against the lavender walls, the shabby-chic touches. Before
I clicked off the lights, I'd look at the tango pictures and think
about my learning curve.

I'm sure I went through the stages of grief, though not neces-
sarily in an orderly way. There was no "there goes denial, here
comes anger, then bargaining, depression, and acceptance."
Rather, they had all merged into the tango stages. The first was
infatuation with the dance and music. This passed quickly, into
the unfortunate stage of humiliation—nobody wanted to dance
with me because I was new. Then trying to recover what little
pride wasn't crushed, I pushed myself to more and more classes
until I could let go of worrying, just a little. Then, instead of
thinking about my dancing, I let myself feel sadness and loss.
Strangely, grief is how we connect with each other and how we
learn compassion; sorrow is what takes us deeply into the human
experience. Innocence is lost, but something better, more complex, can come from experience. But I wanted more than just a
tough-love lesson. I wanted to be better than before my breakup.
I had a hunch that tango could lead me to that place as well.

Claire and I signed up for a four-hour followers workshop
with a tanguera who was visiting from Buenos Aires. She was
known as "La Leona" (the Lion). Most professional tango dancers are bone-thin, and many are beautiful or at least striking.
To my surprise, La Leona was short and thick-waisted. She had
probably never been classically pretty—her face was almost

masculine, with thick lips and puffy eyelids. Her hair hung around her face in a jagged shag cut. She sat on a stool, slightly slouched over, and pulled the edge of her T-shirt down as she spoke to the crowd of women who had gathered.

"I will tell you when you have permission to videotape the lesson," she said. "Please don't do it before then. Now, get in partners. This is what I want you to do." She demonstrated on her assistant, hooking one hand up between the woman's breasts and grabbing her by the bra. With her other hand she pulled up the top of the woman's underpants, right above the pubic mound, and tightened her grip.

"Now," she said. "One of you, grab the other like this and walk in the line of dance."

There was a very awkward moment, when we had to decide which one of us would grasp the other by her undergarments, and twist them and yank them up in this rather barbaric manner. I faced my partner, a small Japanese woman, and she smiled.

"You can lead first," she said.

So I bunched up her bra and underwear. The music started and I led her around the room. I actually enjoyed leading—there's more creativity involved than in following—and it seemed easy to give her pleasure, make her smile. And I was always right—she had to follow me no matter what fool thing I did. Ahh, the world from a man's perspective. The navigating was tricky, though. I had to watch out for other couples awkwardly making their way around the room. After one song we switched, and the followers now grabbed the leaders by the bra and panties. I wasn't sure what it was supposed to feel like or what the lesson was about, so I just focused on the lead. She was soft but strong, and we wove through the crowd, laughing occasionally as we almost bumped other couples.

Claire was dancing with Marcel's girlfriend, and as they passed, Claire said, "I bet you never pictured this when you signed up."

The song ended and we gathered around La Leona, who was perched on her stool.

"So I want to know what you thought about, your legs or your tits?" she asked.

Women in the class murmured responses.

"The point is that it feels so awkward that you don't think about your legs, but rather your chest," she said. "That's where you dance from, that's where you find your power." She demonstrated how to prepare your core to dance. "Breathe in, like the air is water filling you up from your vagina, up the rib cage, to your chest," she said. As we worked on this, she walked around the room and told us to put our hands on her torso while she inhaled.

I placed my hands on her fleshy mid-section and felt the transformation, as if she elongated inches, and her core transformed into an animated force.

"This will help you all find your inner Lion, your own Leona," she said. "In Buenos Aires the women find their lion before they leave their house. As they dress, they are preparing their attitude. Your Leona helps you protect your territory. Your legs belong to your leader—but you must maintain a balanced core and a sense of self."

We moved on to learning embellishments, the taps, dragged feet, and quick swivels a woman can do between steps. La Leona told us that we could turn on our video cameras and record her. She held on to the back of a folding chair and demonstrated possible embellishments that could happen during a forward ocho. Suddenly this squat, homely woman was transformed into a dancer so graceful and articulate that she became beautiful. The fluidity and strength of her movements were stunning as she swung a muscular leg behind her in a circle, whipped it forward, then let it land on the floor as if it were weightless.

Before class ended, she gave us tips for social dancing. "Watch the leaders to see who you want to dance with. Don't judge on appearances," she said. "One of my favorite dancers used to be a little old man; he must have been over seventy years old. He made me feel like I was falling in love. But—and this is important—you need to love yourself enough to say no to bad dancers."

The following Sunday Claire and I went to Dario's class.

Marcel teased us as we walked in. "*Las Leonas* are here," he said.

Jokingly, I hissed at him and formed my hands into claws.

Dario hushed us and started teaching the lapiz.

For the lapiz, or pencil, you drag your foot in a circle, as if you were drawing in the sand; the foot never leaves the ground. The lapiz is a motion that can be gentle, reminiscent of a finger tracing a cheek, or it can be done with aggression, more like a bull pawing the ground before charging. The follower can do it by herself during a pause, but when both dancers in the couple make a slow circle together, keeping their bodies still and just moving their feet in concentric circles along the floor, it can be very sensual—a suspended state of seduction.

When the man stops a woman's foot with his, then slowly brings it back across the floor with his foot, it's known as *la arrastrada*, or "the drag or sweep." It's hard to pinpoint the sensuality of this step. It might be in the feigned resistance of the follower: The leader pushes the follower's foot across the floor, never losing contact. But the essence could also be found in the possible reciprocation as the follower, in an unaccustomed show of willfulness, drags her foot back. This, like almost all steps, is supposed to be led; but some followers initiate the sweep back, and some men like the forthright gesture. It's daring, a little provocative, and even sexual in its undertones.

We rotated around the circle—leaders moving forward by one place each time—and practiced our sweeps. The class, a typical cross section of young and old, male and female, practiced dragging their partner's feet across the floor. Some concentrated on the steps, others cracked jokes, and Dario walked among the couples commenting *"Eso es"* or *"No, como así."*

A few leads didn't like it if I back-led a little, but they pretended to be fine with it, wearing a tight smile that betrayed irkedness. Perhaps they'd had trouble with willful women before; maybe that's why they danced tango—they got to be fully in charge. Maybe their masculinity was threatened. Still others couldn't abide this back-leading at all and would retort, "You have to wait to be led." But some men liked it when I did it a little. At that moment the dance steps felt like flirtation—both of us were participating equally. Domination and submission were not part of it; it felt, well, like dancing. There is no telling beforehand which man is okay with a proactive woman—age, size, and nationality don't provide clues.

The dynamics of the lead-and-follow relationship changed during tango's revival in the 1980s. This is often credited to a couple, Juan Carlos Copes and María Nieves Rego. Dance partners from Buenos Aires, they married, then divorced but kept dancing together. Copes and Nieves produced the show *Tango Argentino*, which opened in Paris in 1983, when the social dance had faded to all but an ember. Night after night the seats sold out and crowds filled the aisles. Other European cities—Venice, Milan, Rome—wanted the show.

In 1985 they came to New York City, and *Tango Argentino* opened on Broadway to rave reviews and an extended run. New Yorkers weren't used to seeing middle-aged dancers. The play showed that sensuality, pathos, and the exhilaration of tango weren't rooted in youth but in experience. This tango was different from the Old World style, with faster, fancier footwork as well as more attitude and more input by the follower. It has been said that María Nieves Rego reinvented the woman's role by subverting the idea that following implies submissiveness. Rather, the woman's personality and will created the dynamic and spark between partners. When beginning the dance, I assumed that every aspect, not just the steps but also the timing, the embrace, and the emotion, was set by the leaders, but I was starting to learn that tango at its very best is an equal relationship.

As we rotated dance partners, Dario walked around the room giving us suggestions. At times he'd stop in front of a student, then lift his eyebrows, smile, and exclaim, "Good." Other times he'd stop and say "No, this way. *Como así*. You must be like, how do you say, a compass, you and your partner's feet pulling together."

When we were pushing each other's feet back and forth, tango felt less like a dance and more like a conversation that borders on a coquettish disagreement. And while tango should flow like pleasant conversation, it can also be power play between the genders and become an insoluble argument. I pushed Allen's foot back with mine, then stepped across him without waiting for a lead so he had to improvise. He smiled, then swept my foot behind my ankle, and I was stuck.

"Help," I said. We both laughed and had to stop dancing to disentangle ourselves. Despite the strict gender delineations and the lead's control over the follower, it really does take two to tango.

As part of my makeover, I decided I was going to stop apologizing when I made a mistake. If I had to say something, I would just exclaim, "Shoot," or for a real mess-up, "Well, crap!" "I'm sorry" was too much of a conditioned response, too little-girlish. I was A Divorcée now—it was time to find my power.

Money had given Josh a sense of power, and that's what I

needed. I had to change my life so that I would not be so close to financial disaster all the time. I had been willing to live the hand-to-mouth life of a freelancer in exchange for having no commitments and having full control over my time. It was too late for me to try and join the corporate world, and I wasn't sure I'd enjoy it. Teaching was so poorly paid that, for me, it just became demoralizing. I found myself reading more and more about entrepreneurs, and I liked their creative spirit.

For several springs since I had moved to New York, I had worked for landscapers installing gardens on rooftops and in backyards of brownstones around the city. It was tough work physically, as we often had to haul bags of soil and saplings up several flights of stairs, not to mention the stress of parking trucks and battling traffic on the city streets. But I loved the transformation. A bare, abandoned space could be almost instantly turned into a little oasis. Clients were thrilled and regularly hugged us when we finished. And the constant tug to be around nature that I'd felt since leaving Alaska was sated somewhat.

One morning I woke up and looked at the tango pictures hanging on my walls and then out the window at the giant condominium being built across the street. Right then I knew what I wanted: to garden during the day and, of course, tango at night. The problem for me in running a business was not pulling together the skills that would be needed but learning to charge clients money. Somewhere along the line, I had internalized the idea that this is rude and unfeminine: A woman should always put others and their feelings and wants ahead of herself. How could I run a business that way?

After the arrastrada class I went to the practica, feeling a little wobbly in my new Comme Il Faut stilettos but overall more confident from my trip to Buenos Aires. I watched Claire and Allen dancing. Claire was a few inches taller than Allen, but they held each other in close embrace. This, too, was a sign of our advancement: We had all stopped fearing close embrace, no longer holding each other at arm's length.

I knew that Claire and Allen were looking for very different things from tango. Claire needed to learn to trust men, to take time out of her stressful life, close her eyes, and let someone else lead. She already knew how to say no to people she didn't want to dance with. "Just do it nicely," she had told me. "Tell them you're resting." Allen wanted to learn how to meet women, to be bolder with them when he did, and he now comfortably approached women standing on the sidelines and invited them to dance.

Some men understood that lack of eye contact means "please don't ask me." I noticed Ear Licker across the room, and he seemed to know to stay away from me; on occasion, I still danced with Sugar Daddy. Some men were absolutely not going to ask me to dance. Tango Whisperer only danced with his long-legged partner. Once, Claire asked the Dominatrix's partner to dance. He curtly said no. She shrugged it off. And there were advanced men who asked me and other beginners to dance. Martial Artist prided himself on his democracy; Hipster mostly danced with advanced women, but he believed a good leader should be able to dance with anyone. Marcel believed in building community by dancing with a wide range of levels. I admired and appreciated these men. Still, I felt I shouldn't have to dance with everyone who asked me — but saying no was so hard.

A short man wearing a triangular veteran's cap asked me to dance. I had been trying to avoid eye contact with him, but he caught me, circling from behind and appearing right next to me. He was about the same age as my beloved grandfather, and I just couldn't say no. He wasn't a student and didn't dance regular tango steps. When I missed a few of his turns, he corrected me. He wasn't even dancing tango, just kind of bouncing along and making sudden turns here and there. After the first song ended he clutched my hand and pulled me into close embrace for the second song. Our feet bumped and he smiled widely at me. I couldn't help but feel angry and a little confused. On the one hand, I should show kindness to this old guy in his little WWII uniform; on the other, why is his experience more important than mine? After the second song I pulled my hand away from his, excused myself, and hurried to the water fountain.

Then Dario turned off the music to make an announcement, and everyone at the practica stopped dancing. A few students protested.

"Will all the beginners here please raise their hands," he yelled. People scattered around the room slowly put their hands in the air. "So now you know who they are."

A man from my class yelled, "And can avoid them."

Everyone laughed.

"No, this is a social dance. A community," Dario said. "You were all beginners once. Dance with them."

This seemed like the decent, right thing to do. It is, however, an issue that hits everyone differently, and it is one that I believed was at the core of the gender struggle.

Josh and I had been having an ongoing e-mail discussion about this. It had started with an offhand comment that he had intended to be humorous. "I sure enjoyed dancing with you, but I got the impression that at times you wanted to lead," he wrote.

Why, when he didn't know the embrace, couldn't hear a beat, and crab-walked around the floor slamming me into people, should he unequivocally be the leader just because he was a man? I couldn't think of an appropriate response, so I didn't reply right away. When he e-mailed me again ("I sense some anger, what's up?"), I replied.

Hi, Josh,

I wasn't angry. It's just odd that men get to lead regardless of their dancing level. I danced with a beginner today, which was fine, but I do wonder why he didn't ask someone from his own class, as there were many women at his experience level sitting on the sideline waiting to be asked. But I guess that's the man's prerogative. Why is it that men still ask women to dance and women have to wait? Just like

*dating—regardless of the changes in society, it's mostly men
who do the asking. As for leaders I don't want to dance with,
I just have a hard time saying "no" to them. And for other
reasons in my life, I need to start saying "no" more.*

*I am starting my own business designing and installing
gardens. I know that the hardest thing for me will be to
charge enough money so that it's worth my time and effort
and, in the end, I don't lose money. Can I learn this from
tango—to not be a martyr to men or to clients?*

Take care,
Maria

Dear Maria,

*Your new business sounds interesting. When you write up
a business proposal I'd be happy to take a look at it.*

*I have been to many practicas where I danced with old
ladies who were just beginning. When I dance with one old
lady, whom no one else wants to dance with, two things
happen. First, she usually clings to me and wants to keep
dancing. Second, other old ladies see this and realize I am
"friendly" and do the same thing. There have been many,
many, many lessons where I have scarcely danced with the
lovely girls that are better dancers. Sometimes, I walk out
frustrated, because there were lots of attractive girls and I
danced with the sweaty grandmas (remember, it is summer
down here). But upon further reflection, my experience was
exactly what it was supposed to be and I gave the greatest
amount of myself to help others.*

From a selfish perspective, my experience was not what I wanted. But from a spiritual perspective, my experience was fulfilling and right. I thought of other people who, due to age, appearance, or ability, were not as desirable to dance with. Hopefully I helped them feel accepted and derive a few moments of pleasure. That is all the good I can do in one day: help someone else feel a few moments of pleasure. This said, I am actually planning on leaving Buenos Aires to travel. This was my original intent, but I became too comfortable. Instead of following the regular, beaten path, I think I may hitchhike to Chile. Many of my friends have told me that I'm crazy, but as my travel adviser, I wanted to see what you thought.

Besos,

Josh

Dear Josh,

As your adventure adviser, I think you should definitely hitchhike. I hitchhiked all over Alaska and with friends through a long stretch in Mexico. You really get to meet people and come to know places. As for the rumors of murders, sexual advances, etc., statistically, you're more likely to get struck by lightning than murdered under any circumstances, and I'm sure you can handle the sexual advances. Usually you get the most rides from truck drivers who want some company—and they will talk your ear off.

As for the tango . . . I admire your selflessness. At this point in my dancing, I like to dance with men who make

*me feel good. There are certain people I have chemistry
with, and we physically match, and I like how they dance.
And usually these men enjoy dancing with me. That is the
goal—that it's a mutually beneficial and enjoyable exchange. I don't want to be a martyr of the tango scene,
and I don't need to be a diva. This is what I want to take
out into the world with me. That I am getting back from an
experience in equal proportion to what I am putting into it.*

   Tango on.
   Maria

In the subtext of our e-mails maybe we were talking about
"us." We had made no plans for the future; it remained unspoken that we would make no effort to see each other. But we
both valued the connection we had made. What I wasn't saying, couldn't ever say to him, was that dancing with him was an
extremely unpleasant experience and it puzzled me because he
was such a great person and very self-aware in other ways. Yet his
bravery astounded me—a total beginner, he went out and asked
women to dance in the tango Mecca of the world. He overcame
his fear of rejection again and again.

Dear Maria,

   *Here is an interesting observation: We have shared a lot,
and for the most part, it was all brought about by tango.
This conversation also was initiated by our shared enjoyment
of tango. Another observation: you have always been more*

advanced than me and as a result, we have never danced tango together connectedly. Yet in the greater realm of life, we have danced a tango for a few months now, sometimes very connectedly, other times out of step. Where our tango goes now depends on our next steps. Fascinating, huh? Have you written a business proposal yet?

BTW: I'm making my way to climb a mountain in the southern Andes.

XO, Josh

A few days later at another practica Claire came over and stood next to me. We chatted about business, or rather, I tried to get information from her.

"At first you always undercharge," she said. "But you learn. Just try not to lose money in the beginning."

While talking we spotted a man circling us. Claire nudged me and said, "Don't do it. Say no to him." Our body language could not have been more discouraging. Both Claire and I had our arms folded over our chests, and we looked away from him. But there is this moment when everything changes to slow motion. From the corner of my eye, he came into closer focus and I saw a hopeful facial expression as he walked a direct path toward us. I geared myself up but didn't want to turn the guy down, so in a rather underhanded move I slipped to the other side of Claire so that he asked her to dance instead.

She said, "No, thank you." The veteran businesswoman was better at this than I was.

"I danced with him last time, and it was horrible," she said. "He told me that he had taken one lesson five years ago. But with an expert tango dancer."

We chuckled a little, and then I whispered, "Oh, no. He found someone." We watched as he led a young woman onto the dance floor. Clearly she was new here. He bumped her feet when he stepped, walked to no discernable rhythm, and then rammed her into another couple.

"It's a train wreck," Claire said. She shaded her eyes with a hand. "I can't watch." We both felt for the woman, as I imagined she was struggling with not wanting to hurt the man's feelings but also really, really hoping for the nightmare to end. "I've noticed," Claire said, "that Irish Guy hardly ever dances. And lately it seems like he does so less and less."

Since my overall experience had improved, I hadn't noticed him as much. But Claire was right. He seemed to prefer to sit in a corner rather than dance. Maybe he was very selective, or maybe he just liked to watch.

"Perhaps he's got a social disorder," I said to Claire. "I'm wondering about some of these people who dance seven nights a week. Don't they have friends? Dates? Family crises?

"That reminds me, any luck finding that guy you were interested in?" I asked her.

"No," she said. "I keep dropping hints to our mutual friend, but nothing."

"I'm going to have a birthday party," I told her. "A big one.

I'm going to break out the wine and the jar of dulce de leche I brought back from Argentina. Why don't you invite him?"

"We could send the invitation to my friend and specifically ask him to bring Xavier," she said.

"Peter agreed to teach a tango class at the party," I told her. "That's what I want for my birthday — my friends to all dance a tango." I spotted Peter across the room and we danced. Osvaldo Pugliese's onomatopoetically titled song "La Yumba" started to play. The beat was crisp and steady, almost military; Peter stepped in short, sharp motions, then from a back ocho he trapped my foot. I started nudging one of his feet until he let me back-lead and sweep it.

In this song the plucking of strings creates a come-hither effect, but then the strong beat returns and you must follow it, relentlessly, until the piano interrupts with a classical riff and everything dissolves, melting into sheer ardor. Peter dropped me into a volcada, and as I swept my leg through the empty space, he righted me onto my axis. Then the clipped beat started up again.

As we danced the basic, Peter whispered to me, "I hope this is okay to say — you've really improved."

"Thanks," I told him. "It's Argentina and my super-sexy new shoes."

"I miss Buenos Aires," Peter said. "I think I have to go back to live there for a while."

"You could revise your screenplay there," I said. "But there's not much paid work because of the crisis."

I didn't want Peter to leave. He wasn't just my friend but also my safeguard. I could show up at a milonga or practica and dance with him for most of the night. On the other hand, when he wasn't there, I was more open to chance; the next man who approached me could be terrible or good. Peter kept me from both. If I was encouraging Josh to ride in the trucks of strangers and hike up mountains, then I should at least be able to brave dance events without Peter.

An instructor, Carlos D., originally from Buenos Aires, asked me to dance. I was intimidated. I thought I might freeze up out of nervousness. He started to press the crook of his arm against my back, and in a slow, deliberate gesture he folded me into the embrace. I made a corresponding motion, pulling him to me with my arm pressing slowly across his shoulders. The song "Poema" (Poem) by Francisco Canaro was playing. Despite the mournful lyrics, the melody is cheerful. *"Fué un ensueño de dulce amor / horas de dicha y de querer. / Fué el poema de ayer."* (It was a dream of sweet love / hours of happiness and loving. / It was the poem of yesterday.)

The dance started well before our feet began to move. I tilted my head down to touch Carlos's forehead. I noticed the pale freckles speckling his bald spot, felt the bulge of his stomach against me. He pulled me to him and held me as though our contours were meant to match—hip meeting hip like pieces of a jigsaw puzzle, chests united as if halves of a whole. Then he worked magic with his feet. He didn't have to travel far. He swept one of my feet in front of the other one, then deftly, smoothly moved the other behind it so they crossed. Then he brought me out with a sweeping step forward and immediately pulled me around him in a tight molinete.

It was challenging and lively but also certain and gentle, with lots of ingenuity. There were no sharp turns or surprises. He never left me wondering, never left me alone. He humbled me, yet made me feel good about it. A follower to the leader, but the leader has to respect his responsibility to the follower. Those realizations, that contract between two people, is where the genders can meet. The argument between men and women blurs in this moment and becomes a truce, then an agreement. This is bliss, and it is why, despite feeling betrayed and bruised, we lick our wounds and then try again at love.

After we stopped dancing, Carlos stepped back and told me, "You can dance tango because you don't fear the embrace. Anything else, steps and techniques, can be learned. But not the embrace. You have that."

I didn't always understand the embrace. I thought about my smudged piece of paper at home, my official divorce. This was my paradox—I had learned the embrace by having my heart broken.

CHAPTER 13

El Abrazo, The Embrace

To PREPARE FOR my birthday party, I had purchased boxes of empanadas from an Uruguayan bakery in Queens, then picked up chorizo and chimichurri sauce from an Argentinean butcher. I found fried *churros* filled with dulce de leche that I planned on serving in lieu of a birthday cake. I bought bottles of hearty Argentine Malbec wine and chilled the white Torrontés I'd brought back from Buenos Aires. A friend who lived in a loft offered to host the party, so we decorated her place with strings of glittering white lights.

Peter had agreed to teach the gathering a tango class, so about half an hour before midnight, we sprang it on the guests. "Thank you all for coming tonight," I announced. "For a present, I would really appreciate it if everyone danced one tango."

First Peter and I demonstrated a dance to the song "Queremos Paz" (We Want Peace), a nuevo tango by the Gotan Project.

Peter, the veteran dance performer, had no problems, but I was so terrified that the thumping of my heart echoed in my ears. He led me through the moves we had practiced during our Friday nights at Triangulo. We stepped together, and he pulled me into a volcada and I swept my foot through the empty space; then he pivoted me into a back ocho and from there he spun me. He turned and I ganchoed through his legs. Then he pulled me against his chest and we returned to a basic. I tried to feel the floor through his shoulder, but it was his heartbeat that calmed my nerves. I rested there for a brief moment, letting my pulse cool down. Then he swept my foot, pulled me against him, and we went back to our basic to finish.

After the song ended, everyone clapped.

"That felt great," Peter said.

I nodded, still a little shaky, and then we herded my friends into pairs.

Grumbles and giggles came out of the group. Some men were following, with women leading. I matched Claire with a friend who was tall enough not to be scared of her long legs, and Allen with a sweet single woman a little older than him. I scanned the room and looked at my friends in the haphazard couplings. They negotiated the embrace, some pulling each other close, others keeping a safe distance. Unlike the tango crowd, I knew intimate details about their lives. The hearts broken by death and divorce, the childhood traumas that continued to haunt, the infertility treatments, miscarriages, cancer diagnoses, disappointments, and fears. And I knew about their happiness: the falling in love, the career switches, the babies conceived, the apartments bought, the new nieces and nephews.

Now I stood in the circle they created, teaching them the embrace, trying to pass on to them some of what I had learned from it.

"Men can pair with men, women with women, it doesn't matter here," Peter said. "But with mixed couples, men, you're the leaders."

"Hey, why do men get to lead?" a friend yelled.

"Okay, you decide who's leading," Peter said. "As you embrace, keep your frame, your upper body straight. Don't hold so tightly that you constrict your partner, but don't be so loose they don't know you're there. Stay solid and steady in your frame."

He pulled me to him. I let my hand gently fall onto his arm.

"This is open embrace," I said. "You maintain the connection through your chests. Keep them parallel." Then I leaned into Peter, wrapping my arm around his back, resting my hand on his far shoulder. "And this is close embrace, your chests pressed together."

"But let's start with practice embrace," Peter said. We demonstrated a basic weight shift, one foot, the other. Then Peter instructed everyone to walk. But the circle was too tight, and nobody could budge. "Okay, we need a circle on the inside," Peter said.

The two lines of dancers moved in parallel circles. Some were bumping, some laughing, some looking into the other's eyes, others nervously avoiding each other. Whether the embrace and walking feels good or awkward and whether it's a song of heart-break or joy, reason or passion, dancing teaches us to be in it fully.

After the lesson ended, Peter played more tango music, and some couples stayed to practice, while others drifted off. I left the dancing to visit with guests. Katherine and Marcus, the couple who had married in Uruguay, were there. They had recently asked me to be godmother to the baby boy they were expecting.

"I want him not to fear women," Marcus told me. "Take him and teach him the tango."

"I'll get him dancing before he even knows what's going on," I promised.

Katherine then pulled me aside and told me some gossip Marcus had heard about my ex. "Supposedly his girlfriend is very jealous," she said. "So jealous he's had to fly home from business trips to assure her he's not having an affair."

I repeated this story to Amy, who also once had a philandering husband.

"This is the fun part," she said. "He's going to cheat on her, too. Guaranteed."

That past week I had gone with Amy to look at wedding dresses. She already knew exactly which one she wanted but tried on a few others first. Then she came to the one, a champagne-gold layered skirt with a slender, corsetlike top. She looked gorgeous in it.

"That's your dress," I had told her. "Stop there or you'll just confuse yourself."

Now Amy looked at the churros on the table, "Just one. The dress will still fit. Right?"

I laughed and went into the kitchen to check on the food and wine. Just then a man with dark hair and sparkling brown eyes arrived at the party by himself. He handed me a bottle of wine to add to the table, but I also noticed he clutched a bouquet of flowers.

"Hi, I'm Xavier," he said. "Is Claire here?" We found her and he presented her with the flowers.

"Umm, thanks," she said.

We learned later that Xavier had been looking for Claire since they'd met and had also dropped hints to their mutual friend. He'd even headed out to a comedy club in the freezing cold while fighting a fever in hopes that Claire would be there, as the comedian was a friend of Claire's.

"There were about four people in the audience," he told me. "The comedian thanked me for my support. I didn't have the nerve to ask about Claire."

So for almost a year, they missed each other; both were too shy to ask their friend directly about the other. Or, as Claire suggested later, maybe the timing just wasn't right yet. The night of my party, Xavier had been settling in to watch a boxing match on television. He had just popped open a beer and decided to check his e-mails one last time before the fight started. He saw the invitation, which had arrived circuitously through a friend of a friend. He quickly showered and changed, stopped for wine and flowers, and headed to the party. But we didn't learn all this until the two of them became a couple. That night Claire didn't even recognize him at first. He had shaved his beard since they'd met, and the party was already chaotic. People bumped into each other as they made their way from the dance floor to the kitchen. One brash young woman was making quite a stir. I had never met her and I never actually interacted with her, but friends kept coming up to me and exclaiming something along the lines of "How do you know her? She's horrible."

Peter approached, miffed. "She told me I don't know anything about dancing the tango. How dare she?"

She smoked pungent, foreign cigarettes and drank straight shots of Patron tequila while she held court, insulting people in the small kitchen. Soon we saw Allen gather up his jacket and the two of them began to leave together.

"Oh, no," Claire said. "Sweet Allen is leaving with that rude woman."

I pulled him aside, "Allen, are you going to be okay?"

"Call us a cab," she demanded. "We're going out now. East Village."

"Don't do it, Allen," Peter said. "It could never be worth it."

"I can take care of myself," he said, and the two of them left, with concerned clucking and comments following them out the door.

"Well, he seems to have lost his fear of women," I said to Peter. "Though, at times, a little fear can be a good thing."

"This would be one of those times," Peter said.

In fact, there were several more hookups that night. One

couple, a Uruguayan man and Jamaican woman who met at the party, became engaged in less than a year. A fellow tanguero shared a ride home with a civilian friend. Later they traveled to Mexico together, fell for each other, and within a few months had a bitter break-up. Such is the nature of the embrace.

Peter and I sat down and took a break.

"I don't know where I want to be," he moaned. "This city wears me down."

I had heard this musing, his complaints and financial worries, so many times.

"My heart's in Buenos Aires," he said.

"Then you should go," I said.

"You think?" he asked.

"You keep talking about it," I said. "I'll miss you, but you may as well try."

As guests trickled out, the volume of the music went up and we danced to disco. Peter had brought a Donna Summer CD, and he started spinning on the dance floor. Someone challenged his sovereignty, so Peter spun, jumped into the air, then landed in a split and bounced while the other dancer dropped to his stomach and wiggled across the floor like an earthworm. We played songs from the *Grease* soundtrack, then more disco, including that old standby, "I Will Survive" by Gloria Gaynor.

I broke away from the dancing and started gathering cups with dregs of wine in the bottom, rumpled napkins, plates sticky with dulce de leche. The party had been a success.

CHAPTER 14

La Salida, The Exit

THAT SPRING I took landscape design courses at the New York Botanical Garden in the Bronx. I bartered with friends: In exchange for my help writing a grant, one designed my business cards; I wrote ad copy for another in exchange for a simple business website. I visited gardens around the city and snapped photos of my favorite plant combinations; I picked the brains of gardeners and designers I knew and applied for a business license.

Between meetings with my own clients, I worked for other gardeners. Many evenings I returned home so filthy and exhausted all I could do was shower and collapse. I was juggling the garden business with writing assignments and still traveled frequently. When I was on the road, I always sought out milongas.

On a chilly night in Helsinki, Finland, I escaped from the

chill blowing off the harbor by slipping into a club where couples wearing plaid flannel shirts clung to each other and danced
tango to a polkalike rhythm. Their particular type of tango was
a little American ballroom, a little Argentine, with a polka hop
and somehow a distinct Finnish flair.

In Phoenix, Arizona, I found a practica going on in a dance
studio tucked back into a mini-mall. Despite the searing summer temperatures, one leader wore full leather, both jacket and
pants. I feared he had put them on in early spring and hadn't
been able to get them off. I avoided him and danced with a
man wearing a white cotton guayabera shirt. He held me so,
so gently, perhaps he thought I might dissolve if he embraced
me too tightly.

In the Mission District of San Francisco, I made my way
past the taquerias where teenage boys and girls clustered around
tables, arguing in Spanish and laughing. Older punk rockers
traipsed by, prostitutes tugged at their tiny skirts, and the nighttime buzz of the city started to accelerate. The art center in the
Mission was a cavernous space that made the crowd seem sparse
even though it wasn't. It had the ubiquitous snack table: some
pretzels, bags of cookies, plastic cups for water, and, against the
wall, the familiar piles of shoes, jackets, and bags heaped under
the seats. At first all the leads avoided eye contact with me, assuming I was a beginner, since they had never seen me before.
So I sat down and rotated my ankle, one then the other, pretending to stretch them out, when in reality I was showing off my
Comme Il Faut shoes, hoping someone would notice that I'd
been to Buenos Aires.

But still I waited; I looked available, ready to return eye contact, but tried not to appear desperate — no smiling at a man first. I sat by myself until a man sat down next to me, introduced himself as Max, and struck up a conversation.

"Are you new?" he asked.

"No, I'm visiting from New York City," I said.

He perked up and asked me to dance. Nuevo music played and Max started stepping faster, challenging me with improvisational steps. He got one foot stuck between mine, so I back-led a bit, sweeping his foot with an arrastra, then stepping over it and giving him a quick gancho.

"Thank you for getting me out of the tight spot and making me look good," he said. "I should just ask now — will you marry me?"

He invited me out to eat afterward, and we went to an all-night diner. A woman with very dark eyeliner and lots of tattoos served us cheeseburgers. Max told me he knew if a follower would be good — in the first three seconds, in fact — by the way she placed her hand into his.

"Impossible!" I said.

"Wipe your hands," he instructed.

I reluctantly put down my juicy California burger and picked up my napkin. When my right hand was less sticky, I placed it in his.

He concentrated for a second. "Gentle, balanced, comfortable on her own axis."

"With a hint of green chili and cheddar juices?" I asked (though I was pleased with the assessment).

Max continued, "I expose my chest, offer my hand for embrace. When she embraces me, I take a breath. If she doesn't breathe, that means she's not responsive. If she does, we're in sync. Then I shift my embrace and expect her to do this, too. It means she's understanding the reciprocity of the embrace."

"Quite a system you have worked out," I said. "Are you ever wrong?

"No," he said. "And by the way, you didn't breathe or shift."

"So was it a bad dancing experience?" I asked.

"Not at all," he said. "It was great."

"Sooo?" I asked.

After eating he walked me out to my car, and as we chatted, he slowly started moving closer to me. I laughed and slipped into my car.

He leaned in the open driver's side window. "Can't you stay here in California longer?" he asked.

In Cuba I stopped into the Casa del Tango in Old Havana and danced with a man who had long arms and elbows that jutted out like a cricket's legs. He had the gnarled hands of a person who once worked very hard. As we danced he whispered, "*Hay que rico*" (loosely, "how nice") into my ear. Later an old woman, wearing a vintage evening gown and blue eye shadow that glittered behind her false lashes, lectured me about men.

"There is the right man out there for you," she said. "But you might not meet him for a little while. Until then, have fun. Date them all, the old ones and the young ones, and when it doesn't work out, dry your eyes and move on."

I met up with friends in Albuquerque, New Mexico. One man I knew there, Mike, tangoed, so we went out to dance. My friends Ben and Marisol joined us; they were swing and two-step dancers. After an hour or so, we left the small group of tango dancers for a country-western bar filled with hundreds of two-steppers, where we all took turns dancing with one another.

During riffs in the music, Ben would start spinning me in turns, pretzels, swings. At times I looked up, trying to soak in the energy of the crowd. The faces were smiling, laughing, the movements determined and yet spontaneous, and I felt that vibration just like on the crowded floors of the salsa socials or tango milongas—when people are connected with each other and the music wraps around them. There's nothing like dancing.

The next day I headed south to the Bosque del Apache wildlife refuge. The Rio Grande had been released to create wetlands for the thousands of sandhill cranes and snow geese. I parked the car and walked to a dock bordering a pond. A crimson sunset spread over the horizon, creating a dramatic backdrop to the camel-colored mountains. The cranes started flying back to the pond to roost for the evening, and the crooked line of birds in flight looked like notes of a musical score. When they landed they stretched and squawked and batted their wings. Then some started dancing, wings lifted, neck arched, and body bowed. They tossed sticks and grass into the air as they pranced.

Nobody knows for certain why cranes dance. It's not for mates or for territory. Some people believe they dance to greet each other, to get to know each other again after a separation, and to align themselves with the universe. Perhaps that's why we dance, as well. As the birds continued to alight on the shallow pond, the setting sun bleeding poetry and drama across the curves of the ridges and rivers, the outlines of mesquite and tamarisk trees, I sucked in my breath and murmured, "Wow," at the unabashed beauty of it all.

I had decided that I wanted to specialize in creating gardens with wildlife habitat for birds, bees, and butterflies. I bought books and studied the best plants for this; there are many, I learned, that are natives to the New York area. I sought out artists in my neighborhood who could make solar-powered water fountains and bat boxes. I found stylish bird feeders and Bauhaus-style modern birdhouses. As for the business side of things, I spent a lot of time on the phone with the state tax department, trying to understand why some services were taxable and others weren't. I was regularly fined for double-parking while I unloaded plants. I had to haggle with clients over money, and at first it made me almost physically ill. I would often toss and turn at night in a cold sweat. But I knew that I was facing my discomfort, and each time it got a little easier.

That first year of my business, between the road trips and the gardening season, I couldn't dance with my usual crowd very often. Still, I tried to make it to the milonga on Sunday nights at the South Street Seaport. Claire was seeing a lot of Xavier, but she also made room for this particular milonga. One balmy evening in midsummer we headed together down to the pier. The enormous masts on the *Peking* rose above the docks like religious symbols, dramatic in the fading light. As twilight spread, a patch of peach sky cut through the gray-hued horizon and the chalky blue river. Lights flicked on, outlining bridges and illuminating rows of rectangular apartment buildings. Tango music drowned out the squawking of gulls, and the port was transformed. The milonga was in full swing.

Claire and I joined a table of people from our studio. Marcel was holding court, pouring beers from a pitcher. One man I had wordlessly danced with very early on, I had learned over time, drove a cab. I liked to tease him when he asked me to dance. "Are you going to be cutting off people and cursing at them on the dance floor?" He always laughed.

"Hey," he asked me. "I've been trying to grow some grape seeds in cups on my kitchen table. Can you give me some advice?"

We all assumed that anonymity made the intimate experience possible, but I loved learning about these people. A man with short-cropped hair with whom I sometimes danced finally told me why he learned the tango. He liked to hang glide but one day flew straight into a tree and broke both his legs.

"It changed me," he said. "I'm an entrepreneur, and now I weigh out all the risks before jumping in. I'm actually a better businessman for it." Immobilized by the accident, he had slipped into a depression. He had been a skier and mountain climber, and he now found his life so unstructured, so unfamiliar that he needed a plan to find his way out of that place. The steps, the music, helped him pull his life back together.

Couples tangoed by us. Dominatrix was kicking ganchos;

Tango Whisperer guided his long-legged partner. The man who had offered to be my sugar daddy danced past with a beautiful auburn-haired woman in his arms. Martial Artist pivoted around his partner. Irish Guy stood off to the side by himself, and Ear Licker had found a platinum blonde to dance with.

Claire and I ordered margaritas. Marcel insisted on paying for them. The spirit was celebratory. A couple who had met at tango lessons had recently married. Also, Dario's wife was pregnant, and he had successfully choreographed and staged a show that mixed modern dance and ballet with tango. Hipster, who had performed in the show, was preparing to move to Buenos Aires and become a serious tanguero. People proclaimed their envy, but he seemed a little sad and protested, "It's not New York. What could be better than this?" He gestured at the ships, the people dancing, the distant lights framed by skyscrapers.

While the music poured out over the dancers, the people at our table laughed and clinked glasses and I realized that I didn't hear only heartbreak in the tango music anymore. There was also intrigue and opportunity, romance and friendship. An upbeat, playful milonga started. I scanned the crowd. Marcel noticed me.

"Peter's not here anymore," he said. "Will you be open to dancing with new people?"

"I'm trying," I said.

"You want to dance with me?" he asked.

"Always," I said. The dj played an even quicker milonga with a crisp 4/4 beat that tapped like the rhythm of a hopeful heart.

We stepped together quickly. The song ended and a faster one began. A man sitting on the side clapped his hands together and shouted encouragement to the dancers, "Yes, do it!"

Argentinean writer Jorge Luis Borges lamented the changes in tango, once full of bravado with lyrics about sexual prowess and knife fights, to the music of heartbreak, or as he put it, when it passed from a display of "braggadocio to sadness." He liked the inherent dueling in the music and dance and believed that milonga music and dance let dancers live the fantasy of bravery and valor. Borges wrote, "I would say that the tango and the other Argentine dance, the milonga, express something directly that poets have often tried to say with words — their sense that a fight can be a celebration."

This place marked my change. I didn't quite recognize myself. I was no longer the lonely, heartbroken woman who had watched this milonga one year ago. In the beginning I needed tango to assuage my pain. During bad times we can choose desolation and become lonely and bitter, or we can choose consolation and reach out to other people. I found consolation in tango, and through it I had dead reckoned myself to a much, much better place.

A cortina interrupted the music, and everyone changed partners. I danced with a man I had never met before. We stood parallel and aligned our feet. I felt the coarse grain of the planks beneath my feet and smelled anchors and rust and barnacles. Seagulls shrieked. The scents of the river and boats mixed with the earthy smells of his hair and skin and sweat. Tango music played and we started to step, hitting half-beats, dragging out pauses that were pulled by the violin and then cut off by the bandoneón. The music engulfed us like a fog, and I found the pulse of his heart as my own softened to match it.

Passersby stopped to watch. Their faces were bemused, impressed, or even a little uncomfortable. Some women nudged their boyfriends, as if daring them to learn. Tourists formed a semicircle around us, and at times I looked up and noticed them. Someone was filming us; someone else snapped shots with his cell phone. Others rushed by, pretending not to notice the hundreds of couples clutching one another.

And every once in a while, I saw a person standing alone—curious and not exactly knowing when or why, but sensing that one day, she would find herself in the arms of strangers, welcoming the warmth of their embrace and learning to dance tango.

GLOSSARY

abrazo   (from *abrazar*, to hug) The tango embrace.

bandoneón An accordionlike musical instrument used by
               tango musicians that originated in Europe.

boleo   (from *bolear*, to throw) With the knees
               together, one leg swings with a whipping
               motion.

cabece   (from *cabeza*, head) A wordless invitation to
               dance at a milonga: Eye contact is made; a
               slight nod of the head follows. If the follower
               accepts, she nods back, if not, she turns away.

cadena   (chain) When steps are done in a repeated
               sequence; the couple usually moves rapidly
               around the floor.

caminita   (from *caminar*, to walk) The tango walk is
                      both backward and forward, with both part-
                      ners balancing their weight with one another.

candombe   Afro-Uruaguayan music and dance; some
                      historians believe it was an influence on or
                      early precursor of the tango.

castigada   (from *castigar*, to punish) When the follower
                      slides her foot down the leader's pant leg,
                      giving him a flirtatious caress.

cortina   (curtain) Nontango music played between
                      tandas at a milonga.

entregarme   (to surrender oneself) The follower gives her-
                      self up to the leader.

gancho   (hook; sometimes used as a verb) When a
                      dancer momentarily hooks a leg sharply
                      around or through the partner's legs.

lapiz   (pencil; used as a verb) Making circular mo-
                      tions on the floor with one foot while at a
                      standstill.

Lunfardo   A type of slang in Buenos Aires that has heavy Italian influence. It was once the language of the underworld, and some claim it was used so police officers wouldn't understand what was being said. Many terms are still found in tango lyrics.

milonga   A social dance, a precursor to the tango, where people gather to tango or dance to a type of lively music written in 2/4 time.

milonguero   (fem. milonguera) A person who frequents milongas and for whom tango is a way of life.

molinete   (windmill; wheel) A step in which the follower walks in a grapevine pattern around the leader, who pivots at the center.

ocho   (eight) Figure eights: a crossing and pivoting figure from which the fan in American tango is derived. El ocho is considered to be one of the oldest steps in tango and refers to a time when women wore floor-length skirts and danced on dirt floors. The quality of women's dancing was judged by the figure eight their skirts left behind in the dirt.

planchadoras   (from *plancha*, flatiron) A woman who sits all night at the milongas without being asked to dance because she doesn't know how to dance well enough.

porteño   (fem. porteña) An inhabitant of the port city of Buenos Aires.

resolución   (resolution) The end to the basic pattern.

sacada   (from *sacar*, to take out) The most common term for a displacement of a leg or foot by the partner's leg or foot.

salida   (from *salir*, to exit) The first steps of the basic tango pattern, or an opening, as well as exit or way out.

tanda   (group, batch) A set (traditionally three to five songs or pieces) of dance music. Usually couples dance together for a tanda. If they aren't dancing well together or one partner isn't enjoying the dance, that person says thank you and leaves before the tanda ends. Tandas are separated by a cortina, or short interlude of music.

tanguero   (fem. tanguera) A tango aficionado who may
                      or may not be a dancer. The term can refer
                      to anyone who is passionate about any part
                      of the tango, such as the music, history,
                      Lunfardo, etc.

vals   Argentine waltz.

volcada   (from *volcar*, to tip over) The leader causes the
                      follower to tilt or lean forward and fall off her
                      axis before he catches her again. Her free leg
                      sweeps the floor.

SELECTED READINGS

WHILE WRITING THIS book, I read and reread *Tango, The Art History of Love*, by Robert Farris Thompson, which provides incredible insights into the evolution of this dance, music, and culture. I learned many things about the tango from Julie Taylor's book *Paper Tangos*. I gleaned lots of information from the book *Tango!: The Dance, the Song, the Story*, by Artemis Cooper, Maria Susana Azzi, Richard Martin, and Simon Collier. And I'm grateful to the Lincoln Center Library for having a copy of *The Tango and How to Do It*, by Gladys Beattie Crozier, in the stacks. *Tango and the Political Economy of Passion*, by Marta E. Savigliana, was not a light read, but an excellent account of the pathos and passion that tango explores in both the personal and the political. *Le Grand Tango: The Life and Music of Astor Piazzolla*, by María Susana Azzi and Simon Collier, as well as *Astor Piazzolla: A Memoir*, by Natalio Gorin and Astor Piazzolla, provided insights into this remarkable musician. As well, stories, poems, and essays by Jorge Luis Borges, particularly the essay *"Historia del tango,"* I highly recommend.

ACKNOWLEDGMENTS

I'D LIKE TO thank the editors of this book, Antonia Fusco and Amy Gash. It really took shape under their guidance. My agent, Jen Unter, has been a constant source of camaraderie in this and other ventures. My family has been encouraging. I'd especially like to thank my sister, Betsey Finn, who read and gave me feedback on the manuscript. Many friends also read the book and gave helpful suggestions and insights. I'd like to thank Joe Wieder, Hayley Downs, Brenda McCarthy, Jill Shulman, and Katy McLaughlin for this. Many, many friends saw me through this difficult period in my life and it made me realize how truly blessed I am. Thanks to all of you.

There are also people in the New York City tango community who made the awkward phases of learning to dance tango a pleasure. I was very lucky to land at the Sandra Cameron Dance Studios and I thank the teachers and fellow students there. My friendship with Renee Turman has been the absolute best thing that has come from tango. I have many fond memories of the nights I spent dancing with Paul Chernosky. I'm a big fan of Dante Polichetti for being a thoughtful dancer and helping newcomers. I will always be grateful to Martín Hernandez for welcoming me and so many others into the community.